Pandemic Moments

Stories of the 2020 COVID-19 Outbreak

Things
Are
Different
Now

Compiled and Edited by Yvonne Lehman

GRACE

Scripture quotations marked ESV are taken from *The Holy Bible, English Standard Version*. ESV® Permanent Text Edition® (2016). Copyright © 2001 by Crossway Bibles, a publishing ministry of Good News Publishers. Used by pemission.

Scripture quotations marked GNB are taken from the *Good News Bible*® Copyright © 1976 American Bible Society. All rights reserved.

Scripture quotations marked KJV are taken from the *King James Version* of the Bible.

Scripture quotations marked NIV are taken from the *The Holy Bible, New International Version*. Copyright © 1973, 1978, 1984, International Bible Society. Used by permission of Zondervan. All rights reserved.

Scripture quotations marked NKJV are taken from the *New King James Version*®. Copyright © 1982 by Thomas Nelson. Used by permission. All rights reserved.

Scripture quotations marked NLT are taken from the *Holy Bible, New Living Translation*, copyright © 1996, 2004, 2015 by Tyndale House Foundation. Used by permission of Tyndale House Publishers, Inc., Carol Stream, Illinois 60188. All rights reserved.

Scripture quotations marked TLB are taken from *The Living Bible* copyright © 1971 by Tyndale House Foundation. Used by permission of Tyndale House Publishers Inc., Carol Stream, Illinois 60188. All rights reserved.

Scripture marked TPT are take from *The Passion Translation*®. Copyright © 2017 by BroadStreet Publishing® Group, LLC. Used by permission. All rights reserved.

Scripture quotations marked VOICE are taken from *The Voice Bible* Copyright © 2012 Thomas Nelson, Inc.
All rights reserved.

Royalties for this book are donated to Samaritan's Purse.

PANDEMIC MOMENTS STORIES OF THE 2020 COVID-19 OUTBREAK

ISBN-13: 978-1-60495-069-4

Copyright © 2020 by Yvonne Lehman. Published in the USA by Grace Publishing. All rights reserved. No part of this book may be reproduced in any form or by any electronic or mechanical means, including information storage and retrieval systems, without permission in writing, except as provided by USA Copyright law.

From Samaritan's Purse

We so appreciate your donating all royalties to Samaritan's Purse from the sale of the books *Divine Moments, Christmas Moments, Spoken Moments, Precious Precocious Moments, More Christmas Moments, Stupid Moments, Additional Christmas Moments, Loving Moments, Merry Christmas Moments, Cool-inary Moments, Moments with Billy Graham, Personal Titanic Moments, Remembering Christmas, Romantic Moments,* and now PANDEMIC *Moments* to Samaritan's Purse.

What a blessing that you would think of us! Thank you for your willingness to bless others and bring glory to God through your literary talents. Grace and peace to you.

Their Mission Statement:

Samaritan's Purse is a nondenominational evangelical Christian organization providing spiritual and physical aid to hurting people around the world.

Since 1970, Samaritan's Purse has helped victims of war, poverty, natural disasters, disease, and famine with the purpose of sharing God's love through his son, Jesus Christ.

Go and do likewise
Luke 10:37

You can learn more by visiting their website at
samaritanspurse.org

Thanks to Penny L. Hunt for the *Pandemic Moments* cover picture. She expressed her gratitude for a book like this and hoped her contribution would strengthen, encourage and bring hope to many in this trying time.

When her four-year-old granddaughter who lives in London — still in lock down mode — cried on the phone telling her everything was different and she didn't like it, Penny wrote the poem on page 9 for her.

Contents

1. *Comments in the Times of Trouble* – Yvonne Lehman...................... 7
2. *Things Are Different Now* – Penny L. Hunt............................ 9
3. *Lessons from a Pandemic* – Andrea Merrell 11
4. *The Real Lessons of Quarantine* – Gina Stinson 14
5. *The Charity of Pasta* – Carrie Vinnedge..............................18
6. *COVID's Test of Love* – Lily Jenkins.................................21
7. *God Is Faithful* – Gwen Hinkle.......................................27
8. *Weeks of Isolation* – Rebecca Carpenter 30
9. *"That Coronavirus Is Bad"* – Melissa Henderson 32
10. *My Pandemic Retirement* – Ann Peachman Stewart 34
11. *Our Only True Stabilizer* – Sherry Diane Kitts 37
12. *Connecting Through Isolation* – Fran Braga Meininger 40
13. *Contentment as Power* – Karen Cook 43
14. *Don't Give in to Fear* – Stephanie Pavlantos 46
15. *Strange Season, Unique Gifts* – Lauren Craft........................48
16. *A Dark and Stormy Night in Quarantine* – Terri R. Miller..........52
17. *Praying Through the Darkness* – L.C. Helms.........................55
18. *Staying Home* – Loretta Eidson......................................60
19. *My Pandemic Play* – Joanne DiRienzo Schloeman 64
20. *Trust God, Even During a Pandemic* – Evelyn Mann 66
21. *No Easter Without Christmas* – Diana Leagh Matthews.............68
22. *Reaching Out* – Cynthia A. Lovely 72
23. *God's Plans vs. COVID-19* – Helen L. Hoover 74
24. *Five Minutes* – Patricia Butler......................................77
25. *More Than a Scrapbook* – Marilyn Nutter 79
26. *A Birthday to Remember* – Diana C. Derringer 81

27. *Finding Joy and Purpose in Seclusion* – Rebecca Carpente 84
28. *Good Friday, Pandemics, and Great Aunt Jorsey* – Martha Hynson 86
29. *Adventures at the Doorstep of a Pandemic* – Heather Roberts...............88
30. *Parting Our Red-Sea Trials* – Alice Klies 90
31. *You'll Never Know How Much It Means* – Jamin Christian Baldwin.....92
32. *About That List* – Cathy D. Dudley 95
33. *Duty and Faith* – Odell Sauls..98
34. *7:00 A.M. with My Dog Freya in the Time of COVID* – Laura Sweeney ..99
35. *Pandemic* – Carolyn Fisher 102
36. *God Thirsts* – Bob Blundell 103
37. *We Got Married* – Alexis Conrad 106
38. *Glorifying God in a Global Pandemic* – Becca Wierwille 108
39. *All Shall Be Well* – Jeri McBryde 111
40. *The Field* – Mindy Gallagher 113
41. *Give Me Liberty, or Give Me . . . COVID?* – Jenny L. Cote................117
42. About the Authors 122

1

Comments In the Times of Trouble

Yvonne Lehman

On December 31, 2019, a strange new pneumonia of unknown cause was reported to the Chinese WHO Country Office. A cluster of these cases originally appeared in Wuhan, a city in the Hubei Province of China. These infections were found to be caused by a new coronavirus, which was given the name "2019 novel coronavirus" (2019-nCoV).

COVID-19 is the name given by the World Health Organization (WHO) on February 11, 2020 for the disease caused by the novel coronavirus SARS-CoV-2. It started in Wuhan, China in late 2019 and has since spread worldwide. COVID-19 is an acronym that stands for **co**rona**vi**rus **d**isease of 20**19**.

-Dr. Sophie Vergnaud, MBBS, clinical expert on GoodRx Research team specializing in pulmonology and internal medicine (posted March 17, 2020)

*

Tuesday, June 9, 2020 — Anthony Fauci, MD, told a group of biotechnology executives that he's surprised by the speed with which the coronavirus has spread across the globe.

"In a period of four months, it has devastated the whole world," Fauci said during a conference held by the Biotechnology Innovation Organization, according to *The New York Times*. "And it isn't over yet."

Fauci, director of the National Institute of Allergy and Infectious Diseases, said a disease like the coronavirus was "his worst nightmare" because it is new, highly contagious, and causes lots of illness and death. Fauci also is a member of the White House Coronavirus Task Force.

"Oh my goodness," Fauci said. "Where is it going to end?" (WebMD)

*

Don't worry about anything, instead, pray about everything. Tell God what you need, and thank him for all he has done. If you do this, you will experience God's peace, which is far more wonderful than the human mind can understand. His peace will guard your hearts and minds as you live in Christ Jesus.

Fix your hearts on what is true, and honorable, and right. Think about things that are pure and lovely and admirable. Think about things that are excellent and worthy of praise keep putting into practice all you learned from me and saw me doing, and the God of peace will be with you.

~Paul (Philippians 4:13–14 TLB)

The mighty God, the LORD, has spoken. . . .
"Call upon me in the times of trouble,
I will deliver you,
and you will honor me."

~Asaph (Psalm 50:1,15 TLB)

2
Things Are Different Now

Penny L. Hunt

I have to wear a mask and gloves
If we go to the store.
But I can give an elbow bump,
And wave, "Hi!" like before.

> Psalm 91:3: God will keep me
> safe from deadly diseases.

My friends cannot come out and play
Bad germs are here and there.
But God is with me every day,
And with me everywhere.

> John 15:15: God calls me
> His friend.

My birthday party's put on hold
And that sure made me cry.
But then I got to stand outside,
And wave as friends rode by.

> Romans 8:28: God works
> everything out in
> a good way.

We go to church inside our car
My school is in my room.
Mom and Dad work from home,
And do their jobs on Zoom.

> Psalm 23:1: God gives me
> everything I need.

I wish that things were still the same,
These changes make me sad.
But God's love is just the same,
And that truth makes me glad.

                                        Psalm 109:26: God's love
                                                    never changes.

Dad says tough times will not last
The germs will go away.
God holds the whole world in His hands,
His love is here to stay.

                                        Matthew 28:20: God will
                                                  always be with me.

3
Lessons from a Pandemic

Andrea Merrell

One day early in 2020, the world was rolling along doing business as usual. Then, without warning . . . everything changed.

Restaurants closed. Only those with drive-thru windows or curbside take-out could operate.

Bank lobbies closed. No one could go in without an appointment — and even then, only one or two at a time.

Hair and nail salons closed.

Churches closed.

Schools closed. Kids were required to do their work online. No graduations. No end-of-the-year field trips.

Movie theaters closed

Ballgames stopped.

Concerts stopped.

No weddings allowed.

Many small businesses, as well as large chain stores, closed their doors.

Parks no longer opened to the public.

And most cities put restrictions on how many people could be together in one place in public. If the number reached ten, the gathering had to disperse.

Even extended families remained apart.

For weeks, the only place to go was the grocery store or drug store, where people wore masks and gloves and stood six feet apart. Paper goods and basic food staples were in short supply. New buzzwords filled the airwaves and social media: *pandemic, corona, COVID-19, quarantine, social distancing*, and *new normal*. A few churches that tried to hold outdoor services were ticketed or attendees threatened with jail.

It seemed the world experienced a lesson in Socialism 101.

Unfortunately, fear became the primary response for many. While the media bombarded the public daily with the (grossly exaggerated) number of deaths from the virus, they failed to report the rise in domestic violence, child abuse, and depression. For many, the world continued to spiral out of control.

But for those who know, love, and trust God, their perspective on life changed for the better. Christians decided to focus on the positive.

There were no school shootings.

Gas prices settled at an all-time low.

For those who still worked or traveled, traffic remained light, with no traffic jams or accidents.

Families spent quality time together and worshiped together. No hectic schedules got in our way. We ate meals at home, practiced better hygiene, and gained a much-needed appreciation for those folks on the frontlines.

Even though the majority of us were confined to our homes, life became simpler. We learned we could live without many of the things and privileges we thought we had to have to survive and be happy.

We all have stories to tell. This pandemic affected each of us — physically, emotionally, mentally, socially, or financially. Some lost jobs. Some lost businesses. Others lost loved ones.

Many wonder if life as we knew it will ever be the same.

For me personally, I've learned through this time that God wants us to slow down. To rest, not only physically, but to rest in Him. Trust Him. Spend time with Him. To spend more quality time with family and be more concerned about others than we are about ourselves. To be content with what we have instead of agonizing over what we don't have. To appreciate life. To be thankful.

We read in Proverbs 16:9 (NKJV), *A man's heart plans his way, but the LORD directs his steps*.

The Passion Translation puts it like this: *Within your heart you can make plans for your future, but the Lord chooses the steps you take to get there.*

God doesn't promise us tomorrow, and He doesn't assure us that everything today will be perfect. But He does promise to be with us and to never leave us. He is our source. Our provider. His thoughts are higher than our thoughts and His ways so much wiser and better than our own.

His plans are to give us hope and a blessed future. He makes beauty out of ashes and turns mourning into dancing.

In *Experiencing God*, Henry Blackaby wrote, "God is *always* at work" — in, around, and through us, even when we can't see or understand. During this crisis many have said that God is up to something. Whatever else God is "up to," I believe He's working in the hearts of His children, teaching us to depend on Him and preparing us for that day of His glorious return.

The future, as they say, remains to be seen. But two things are certain: COVID-19 did not catch God by surprise, and He never wastes an opportunity to teach His children and draw them closer to Him.

Maybe each of us should ponder what He's doing in our heart — and consider what lessons we have learned and will learn from this pandemic.

4
The Real Lessons of Quarantine

Gina Stinson

I was sitting in a hotel room casually watching the news with my children when I heard the words, "coronavirus," for the first time. After seeing the images coming out of China, my son looked over at me and asked if that was going to make it to America. I chuckled and said a very confident, "No."

Yet two and a half weeks later we found ourselves under quarantine. I had been sorely mistaken.

In Texas, precautions were put into place quickly, shutting down all but "essential" businesses. In just a few days' time, toilet paper, hand-sanitizer, bleach products and various household groceries were scarce. My family grabbed a package of toilet paper and bottled water anytime we went to the store. When restaurants were closed, we began eating all of our meals at home, and for more than fifty-seven days in a row, we ate from our own kitchen.

During the first government-induced shutdown, essential businesses did not include churches. With the stringent stipulations, it would have been nearly impossible to have kept the doors of churches open during this time.

But even though the doors were locked, it didn't mean the Church was not at work. Drive-through food banks, Mother's Day gift distribution and even a church vote for a new youth pastor happened during this time.

Online Bible studies, Zoom meetings and online services through YouTube and Facebook became the norm for most churches.

God's people learned to navigate the virus, and in my little world — in small-town Texas — we were surviving. There was a spiritual urgency that was refreshing and exciting. There was a hunger for God, a genuine seeking for Him that I had never seen. My pastor-husband never missed an opportunity to talk with people who contacted him about their anxiety, fears, and uncertainty during this time. Some needed a shoulder, others needed salvation.

As I write this, the coronavirus has a new name, COVID-19. It's not over. In fact, now we are regulated to wearing masks, social distancing, and other attempts at slowing this pandemic down. Though we had been allowed a short furlough with small limitations, it would seem that we are headed back to more restrictive ways of living in the near future. It's an uncertain time.

*

At what I thought might be the peak of the pandemic I wrote this:

> My kids are getting a day off today. No chores, no school, no waking up early. No, they aren't sick. They aren't ahead in their schoolwork — in fact, quite the opposite. This year has been a rollercoaster for our academics. There is no chance we will recover all that was to be learned in the 8th and 12 grades.
>
> And guess what? It's all ok.
>
> They aren't going to be delinquents or idiots. They aren't going to mooch off the government and welfare system because they had a less-than-ideal year of school. Those are character issues, not academics.
>
> Taking a day off of school to let them breathe, catch their breath, chill, rest, play, be creative, or do nothing will be good for them and me.
>
> Friends, this is a hard time for kids and for adults. Some personalities handle things better than others

but after over a month confined, most of us realized this isn't a staycation or a sabbatical. This is work in a whole different way of doing things than we have done it before. It's cooking, cleaning, teaching, studying, managing, stressing, budgeting, planning, loving — in new and different ways. And sometimes we just need to take a day off and rest. Requiring nothing of ourselves. We will be better for it and so will our families.

The schoolwork isn't going anywhere.

The dishes will wait.

The laundry will multiply regardless.

Twenty-four hours of cereal, hot pockets and popsicles might not be ideal but it won't kill them.

Give yourself and your kids some grace and space. That's my plan for today. Just a little room to breathe . . . tomorrow we can get back to math and history and chores and all the stuff.

Today is for rest.

Even youths grow tired and weary, and young men stumble and fall; but those who hope in the Lord will renew their strength. They will soar on wings like eagles; they will run and not grow weary; they will walk and not be faint.

— Isaiah 40:30-31

I will refresh the weary and satisfy the faint.

– Jeremiah 31:25

*

You see, the virus has slowed the world down. Travel is restricted, school is at home, families are eating around the kitchen table, and parents are working from home. We can either embrace this opportunity to soak in what God wants us to, or we can complain about the things that we are missing out on. So much of what I have learned on this COVID-journey is that perspective is everything. The glass can be half full or half empty . . . and most of the time that is determined by how I look at things. How we act and react has an impact on our children.

Some days we may need to just rest.

Jon Acuff, a well-known Christian, motivational speaker and author, posed a question early on in the pandemic. He asked, "What do you want to look back ten years from now and say you accomplished during the pandemic?" I decided that day I didn't want to waste the time. If God prompts me to rest during this time, I want to obey. If He calls me to serve, I want to serve. If He calls me to support, cook, write or work — I want to obey.

Shouldn't that be our heart always? Maybe the lessons of COVID-19 are farther reaching than good hand washing, social distancing, and face masks. Maybe in stripping away so much of the normal in my life, God is simply calling me to obey.

5
The Charity of Pasta

Carrie Vinnedge

In the beginning . . .
the word "Pandemic" was scarier than the illness itself.

Pandemic was a Hollywood movie with actors in hazmat suits saving the last of mankind. Then the apocalypse and a lone survivor fighting zombies.

The COVID-19 virus was just a bad flu.

Why were people escalating it to crisis proportions?

*

I was a stay-at-home mom with an empty nest. My husband did virtual engineering. We worked from home. We tracked the news of the virus from home and wondered why the rest of the world had so easily lost their minds.

Before there was substantive information about this threat, there was fear. Fear was not a good look for America.

It was the impulsive behaviors to be masked from death that scared me.

The media said the sky was falling. It felt like an irrational obedience for everyone to surrender their livelihoods and their free will — to stop breathing natural air. Where was the push-back? Where were the stats, the skeptics, or the patriotism? I grieved because instead of responding with discernment, my country chose to react emotionally.

How else is a manic craze for toilet paper explained?

I never knew what it felt like to not be allowed to attend church. It was awful and confusing. I was both resentful and distressed. How dangerous was this virus?

Before the tally of days in quarantine had reached double digits, information was everywhere. Opinion became fact, news was biased. Billboards went up saying we were "all in this together." Every aspect of life involved COVID-19.

It was a deeply troubling, unnatural burden. I didn't want to live in fear. I didn't want to be separated from my loved ones. I didn't want to be criminalized for trusting God and seeking wisdom. I didn't want to be hated.

I didn't want to talk about it anymore.

I was not strong. I prayed to go out with an attitude of love — something to give, to help. It was quiet and grim at the grocery store. Everyone was serious. I was quiet too.

I don't want to shove for the last box of pasta.

There was a quiet in town, in deserted streets. But I felt the undercurrent of hysteria like a high, thin pitch, and base notes out of sync.

I stayed home in my bubble.

One morning I took my journal to the back patio, spending time with my Lord. It was good to hear the birds. It was wonderfully quiet, the way the whole neighborhood was on a Saturday.

I also heard the airplanes ascending; it meant germs were going other places. Who was taking them and to where? I prayed for those who took the risk. Whatever the reason, it must be urgent.

Would crisis come to my home? My family?

There was a birthday to celebrate. Some of my children came with their spouses. One, with his wife, chose to distance instead. The burden turned bitter with our differences. We were not our best selves. Sometimes I thought if I got the virus, I could guilt everyone to forgive each other.

The push-back came. The COVID-19 crisis made way for social

injustices to go viral as well. The turmoil in the world, in our nation, stepped up so high the sky was no longer falling, it was being torn down. Bare hands looted and fought and spray-painted individual rights across the walls of burning buildings. It was a fighting country. If one was not angry about this virus or that trespass, then their insensitivity was offensive.

I wanted to carry a sword and say that I had slain evil. When I turned in that direction, it did not bring joy.

*

The crisis of COVID-19 made me realize how important it is to nurture joy. Being in harmony with God brings joy. Jesus endured the cross (and so many other persecutions) for the joy set before Him. The joy of the Lord is my strength. I delight in Him because I am not strong.

I like birthday cake and giving presents. I like singing praises in a church full of friends. I like riding with the car top down and smiling at people. I want to see all the faces unhidden. Maybe I am insensitive to say so out loud. But then, aren't there enough angry people?

Life is a vapor. Before it vanishes live wisely, forgive generously, share a meal with your neighbor — there is certain to be enough spaghetti to go around.

6
COVID's Test of Love

Lily Jenkins

Ever since my sister and I marched Barbie down the aisle to marry Ken, I had a vision of what my wedding would look like. As my life developed, I began to believe that dream would never happen for me. My future husband did not magically appear in college. He did not show up at my workplace. He didn't materialize in law school. He wasn't at church; he wasn't in the courthouse; he wasn't anywhere.

At age thirty-two I became resigned to my fate as the lovable spinster aunt. Then a man named Jamie walked into a singles mixer picnic on July 27, 2019 with a watermelon on his shoulder. He talked about his work in IT and about his travels to Ecuador and about his love of swing dancing. I was fascinated. I played aggressively at musical chairs to capture his attention. I yanked the chair out from my opponent at the last second, and it worked. As I left the picnic, he chased me down and asked me for my phone number — to give me more information about swing dancing.

So sparked my first deep and lasting romance. I was wary and afraid to let my walls down, but Jamie was patient and kind and showered me with chocolate, flowers, apples, restaurant dining, adventurous outings, and compliments. Slowly, steadily he won me. Our first kiss was in November, and after that, I never looked back. As we celebrated Christmas, I could hear the distant sound of wedding bells chiming.

Sometime in January, we began talking about the future — we talked about plans. We talked giddily of being in love. Then, at the end of

January, Jamie developed bronchitis.

We spent two weeks apart and were about to be reunited on Valentine's Day, but there was a catch . . . I had been feeling tired and had a sore throat. I had even gone to see my doctor because it hurt so much. They quizzed me about whether or not I'd been to China's Wuhan province — a coronavirus prevention measure — and then they let me in for my appointment.

It turned out that I had mononucleosis: the kissing disease.

The doctor told me I shouldn't kiss Jamie for a month. I sat in my car, feeling robbed. My first Valentine's Day with a date and I couldn't kiss him? I went home to wallow in my bad luck.

A friend encouraged me to put on a fancy dress and do a Skype date. So, I did — to good effect. We spent hours chatting and flirting and laughing together. Valentine's Day had been redeemed.

Jamie spent the next two weeks on a campaign to heal me — and himself. He was still coughing from his bronchitis. He sent me to a massage therapist three times and brought me food, chocolate and flowers. I fell deeper in love. We began talking about getting married. It was so obvious we should.

After the month expired, despite fear of COVID-19 floating in the atmosphere, we went to the grounds at Biltmore Estate to enjoy a picnic together, and nice long kisses. I was hoping he would propose. But it wasn't time yet.

As the restrictions rolled out, we had to adapt our dates. We could not go to a concert, or have private dance lessons, or go to a renaissance festival. But we could take long walks, make each other home-cooked meals, and watch our favorite movies.

We kept talking about marriage. Jamie explained he wanted to propose and give me a fine ring, but there were no jewelry shops open.

The next time I visited my forthright grandmother, she demanded to know why I wasn't engaged yet. With equal frankness, I told her. Grasping the situation, she bolted from her chair and went into her bedroom to rifle through her jewelry boxes. "Listen," she said. "You can't let that stop you. You all need to borrow a ring from somebody and move on with it!" She wanted to offer her own ring for me to wear, but it was much too large. Still, I took her wisdom and shared it with Jamie.

We selected a stand-in ring from Amazon.com to tide us over until the shops opened. Then, on April 17, 2020, Jamie and I traveled to a waterfall. We went behind it, and he spoke into my ear above the roar of the water. He told me that I made him a better man, and that he loved me with all his heart and from that day forward I would be his chosen love. Then he dropped to one knee and asked me to marry him.

I nodded happily and yelled, "Yes!"

As we embraced, Jamie mentioned that he had been torn about whether to get a photographer but had decided to keep the moment private for just us.

As he was speaking the words, I noticed a rather large man walking down the path toward the waterfall, and in his hand he was wielding a professional-grade camera. I smiled. Perfect timing.

We asked the man if he would take our picture because we had just gotten engaged and he eagerly agreed, getting many beautiful angles of us. Afterwards, Jamie spread out a romantic picnic for us and presented me with a dozen red roses . . . twelve construction paper hearts.

Twelve of them!

He had me hold the bouquet and instructed me to select one rose. I did, and he read from one of the hearts about one of his favorite moments from our love story. He had written out a treasured memory on each rose.

Jamie and I eagerly set a date: May 30, 2020. Enthusiastically, I went about ordering invitations and mailing them at lightning speed. Life was a flurry of wedding planning. Most vendors were eager to help us, but also hamstrung by stay-at-home and closure orders. The rental company for the tent I wanted to rent for the outdoor reception wouldn't agree to the contract until stay-at-home orders were lifted.

Bakers made us samples of cake and left them by the front door of their establishments so we could grab and go. Jamie and I prayed and hoped that businesses would be allowed to do some normal activities on May 8th. The government eased up, right when we needed them to, in order to stay on track for the wedding. We managed to get a private appointment with a jeweler the evening of May 8th when North Carolina allowed business to open under limited conditions.

Everything was going fine . . . up until the eve of my open-house-styled bridal shower on May 16th. Jamie and I met that Friday afternoon to go on a hike. We were both feeling stressed. Jamie was run down from some long, intense hours at work, and his cough was still hanging on. We decided on a nice, four-mile hike to work out the frustrations. Unfortunately, the trail was six and a half miles. It ate up more of our evening that we wanted it to.

On the way home, Jamie remarked that he was cold. By the time we returned, he asked to borrow a sweater. I felt his forehead and found it very hot. Concerned that his bronchitis had come roaring back, I wrapped him in a sweater and then more blankets upon his request. I monitored his fever level and kept a cold rag on his head. Eventually, his fever broke.

I drove up to my mother's house for the shower the next morning — all the while concerned about Jamie. Dear friends came by and chatted for a few minutes on the front porch, mindful of social distance. Afterwards, we had a nice meal on the back deck with my family and Jamie's mother.

On Sunday evening, Jamie reported he was feeling better. In the days that followed, he got himself tested for COVID-19, and the test came back positive. The news hit me like a wave of ice-cold water. We faced quarantine — apart from each other for two weeks. He developed more intense symptoms, coughing so much in the first few days he could barely carry on a phone conversation. I felt helpless. All I could do was order him door-dash soup from Chik-fil-A and send a humidifier to his apartment.

Then, my test came back positive as well. Thankfully, I felt no symptoms, but it was clear to me that with eleven days left to go, I was going to have to cancel the wedding.

I must have made two hundred phone calls. I had to contact the people who had come to the bridal shower and let them know. People that I had seen following my exposure to Jamie scrambled to get tested. I miserably waited for their results, hoping and praying for the best, while I tried to stay healthy by sleeping and consuming vitamin supplements.

Surrounded by tulle and decorations, I slipped into a mild depression. It wasn't fair. I had waited so long for my wonderful love story to happen. I had met an amazing man who treated me like a queen, and when I was on the verge of having my dream wedding, COVID-19 had ripped it to shreds.

The domino effect on people quarantining themselves, and the disruption in many lives that followed, shook me to my core. God showed me that I had been so focused on my own wedding, my own story, that I had lost sight of the stories of my friends and loved ones. They endured a lot of worry and concern due to the threat of exposure. I couldn't do that to them again!

After a week went by, Jamie started feeling better. We began talking and praying about what to do. We decided to limit our wedding to family and bridal party only and live-stream the wedding for the other guests. We didn't arrive at the decision in one conversation. We both had to release our dream of a big wedding. But it was clear to us that we didn't want to wait months for conditions to improve before starting our lives together.

As we looked at the calendar, we tried to balance some considerations: availability of the minister, the length of time we had left before our marriage license expired, and avoiding holidays. We decided on June 27, 2020 which happened to be my parents' wedding anniversary.

In a way, Jamie and I were given a gift. The challenges of COVID-19 bound us together and forced us to work through adversity. We know our love runs deeper than positive tests and quarantine. We got a chance to examine the inherent beauty of a simple wedding ceremony — where the focus is on the bonding of two lives together forever.

It wasn't a Barbie and Ken wedding, but it was something much better — a simple, profound testament to the strength of our love and a declaration that even in difficult times we can pursue happiness.

7
God Is Faithful

Gwen Hinkle

Life was moving along at a nice clip until COVID-19 descended upon my community. As a home health nurse, I am trained to handle a lot of medical issues, but nothing could have prepared me for a world-wide pandemic.

When Oregon's governor put in effect the mandated Stay at Home Order, it became apparent to me that this was actually happening, and I was going to have to take care of patients with coronavirus.

New routines were put in place to prevent the spread of the virus. I did daily checks with work on my temperature and whether I showed any symptoms of the virus. Wearing a mask and face shield became a normal occurrence while doing visits with my patients, despite the frustration of my glasses and the shield fogging up and impairing my vision. Daily cleaning of the inside of my car, bags, and shoes became tiring and the smell of Pine-Sol became repulsive to me.

I became a member of the COVID Team instituted by my agency to designate a group of clinicians who would see all the COVID-19 patients in their homes. This required me to be fitted for an N-95 mask, but wearing the mask wasn't as easy as I thought it would be: I quickly discovered that I could not breathe through my nose very well due to a narrowing in my right nostril. But with all the creative thinking we had to do during this time, I was able to solve that problem by using nasal strips.

There was a procedure in how I donned and doffed my PPE

(personal protective equipment) gear at my car. Besides wearing a mask and shield, I was required to wear a yellow gown and booties. A "PPE Buddy" was assigned to me to help ease my way as I struggled to find a system that worked best for me.

My patients commented that I reminded them of Darth Vader because the mask and shield made me sound like I was in a tunnel.

My heart was burdened as I heard about the many lives lost to this pandemic. No one could have foreseen this tragedy. The crazy virus gave no warnings and it was impossible to predict how it would affect people. A person's age didn't matter; the virus seemed to randomly affect each person differently. Some individuals had no signs of the virus while others showed mild symptoms. Then there were folks who were affected so badly that they had to be placed on ventilators for weeks.

At home I became the designated grocery shopper for the household while also sequestering myself from my parents, who live with me, to keep them safe.

I had no personal contact with anyone unless I wore a mask. No hugs. I was missing the social interaction that I normally thrived on.

What made this time difficult was when the anxiety started to gurgle up inside me, causing great stress to my body. Sometimes I would cry between patient visits, trying to release the pressure that had built up.

I had reached my boiling point of COVID-19. My heart, soul, and mind felt like a drought. The anxiety got so bad that it displayed itself one day when I was talking with my supervisor and suddenly I cried out, "I miss my friends!"

Of course, my little outburst took my boss by surprise. He quickly addressed the problem by saying, "Please, take a few days off and go see your friends. Come back refreshed so you can do your job effectively."

Managing the stress and anxiety became a priority. All I could think about was how I needed more of God. So, I changed some habits. It's amazing what a difference it made when I started out the day exercising and listening to praise songs. Just taking time to be still and lifting my hands in the presence of the Lord gave me strength that carried me through the day.

I began to eat healthier. I took vitamins.

Mom gave me verses on sticky notes to post in the car to remind me who was in control.

I have awesome friends and family who surrounded me with encouragement and prayers. I have no words to express how much this meant to me. When God says He is for us and will *never* leave us, He is not kidding.

One of the sweetest moments during this time was taking a break and seeing one of my friends. We laughed so hard it was like applying a balm to my hurting soul. Basically, we did whatever suited our fancy. When I came back home, I was refreshed and regenerated, ready to tackle COVID-19 again.

My patients were always appreciative that someone would come out to see them.

The most blessed thing I witnessed was how people came together during this pandemic. Was this God's way of saying, "Hey my children, I love you. Love each other as yourself; care for each other. Don't forget I am here with you."

Why does it take a tragedy to wake us up and reach out to God? I don't know. But I hope that this world never has to go through this again. 2 Thessalonians 3:3 (ESV) tells us *the Lord is faithful. He will establish you and guard you against the evil one.*

The pandemic has taught me that God is with us no matter what and that He will *never* leave us.

Now, how cool is that! God is faithful.

8
Weeks of Isolation

Rebecca Carpenter

With every sun's rising, surprise us with Your love,
satisfy us with Your kindness.
Then we will sing for joy and celebrate every day we are alive.
-Psalm 90:14 Voice

Two weeks of intense fatigue from bronchitis kept me housebound. Just as I improved and looked forward to getting out, the coronavirus pandemic added more time of isolation.

When I first recovered from bronchitis, energy returned and I eagerly attacked chores around my house. I cleaned out closets and the garage. My yard looked better after I pulled weeds and trimmed plants.

Each day I read, finished craft projects, played games, called and texted friends, sent cards. . . .

Then my focus wavered. My to-do list stared at me defiantly when I glanced its way. My mind formed plans but motivation disappeared.

For a few nights, sleep came sporadically. One day I got up at 3 A.M., read the Bible and my daily devotions. After praying, I slipped back into bed for a couple more hours of sleep.

Later that morning clouds muted the sky but no rain came for the parched earth. However, the peacefulness of the lake consoled me. Bird songs revitalized my sapped energy.

Suddenly, boisterous squealing and screeching from one side of the lake to the other disturbed the tranquility. A bald eagle swooped from one treetop to another.

I grabbed my binoculars and focused on the majestic bird. A next-door neighbor appeared with her binoculars too. As we scanned the lake, we noticed two adult eagles far apart in pine trees.

Another neighbor joined us and we all peered into the forest to find the source of the desperate cries. Earlier a young eagle perched at the edge of its nest. The parents were nearby, encouraging the youngster, but not helping him fly. No matter how much he cried out, he had to do it on his own.

We didn't see the young one fly, but after several minutes, silence returned.

From chaos to serenity, the episode revived me as I connected with my neighbors. We looked at caterpillars and butterflies in a butterfly garden. Each of us had planted milkweed for Monarch caterpillars. We enjoy the wonder of their metamorphosis.

Like the shrieking of the adolescent eagle, whining doesn't change my situation. Instead of complaining about being home, I can make the most of isolation. While stuck at home, I have seen more of my neighbors as we meet in our yards. On daily walks and bike rides, I encounter old friends and make new ones. I have learned from shows on the History Channel and enjoyed creating new crafts. I am cooking and baking more.

Each day, I can choose how I will react to my situation. Will I whine, or will I be thankful?

Dear Lord, help us as we deal with difficult situations. We know You are near even during the trials when we feel alone. Help us be thankful. Amen

9
"That Coronavirus Is Bad!"

Melissa Henderson

The year 2020 began with familiar sights and sounds. Resolutions, plans for family trips to celebrate special occasions, work goals, and a fresh perspective to make this year a great one. These thoughts were not new. The year was new.

Then . . . the alerts began on television, radio and social media. A virus was causing severe illness in every state. No cure was known. The number of people with the sickness rose every day. The death count began and grew larger with every hour. Sadness, despair, fear of the unknown reached from coast to coast.

Checking social media, all I could find was doom and gloom. Schools closed. Restaurants closed. "Social distancing" became the new catch phrase. Authorities advised everyone to stay at least six feet apart. I kept saying when the virus was gone, the term "social distancing" would probably be added to the dictionary.

The public was asked to stay home and if we had to go outside of our homes, to wear a mask.

Next came the mask shortages and other medical supplies shortages. Health care workers were exhausted beyond anything they had experienced in the past.

More doom and gloom.

When our two-year-old grandson asked why he couldn't go to preschool and see his friends and teachers, our son and daughter-in-law explained there was a bad virus making people sick. Everyone needed to stay home.

Often people will say that a two-year-old child won't comprehend something so serious. Yes, children understand much more than we think. Children absorb their surroundings and when we are upset and worried, they feel the tension and concern.

My husband and I enjoy having "video chat" with grandson Rowan. He loves to see our faces and we love to see him. The video calls are usually full of laughter and talk of dinosaurs or cars and trucks. His imagination is amazing.

One evening, during our video chat he shared, "That coronavirus is bad!"

We agreed. "Yes, that coronavirus is very bad."

Even at two years old, this child can feel the emotions of the adults around him. He and other children don't have to know all the details to know there is worry and concern for others.

My husband and I are proud of our son and daughter-in-law. They share with Rowan about daily life. He doesn't need to know all the details of the sickness and death around him. He knows enough to understand there is a reason why he can't go to preschool or see his friends.

I thought of all the other children in the world. How were they handling the news they heard? Were they scared? Did those children have parents, grandparents or other loving family members who could comfort them and remind them of God's love?

Some children and adults may have difficulty showing their true feelings. They may keep their thoughts bottled inside.

When viruses, other illnesses, tragedy and sadness happen in our lives, we must remember to consider the feelings of others. We each deal with circumstances in unique ways. Praying for each other and offering a listening ear or a shoulder to lean on can change someone's life.

When our grandson shared, "That coronavirus is bad!" I was reminded how he is being taught to care for others and share the love of God. He is already filled with compassion and care for those people around him.

A precious two-year-old child can show love.

I pray we all show God's love to each person we meet.

10

My Pandemic Retirement

Ann Peachman Stewart

I didn't want to retire. As the magic year loomed, God and I engaged in discussions. I loved my job and the people I worked with. I felt excitement every time I entered the retirement home, because we made a difference. We not only set precedents in the way we served our elders, but looked for ways to change the face of eldercare throughout the province, the country, even the world. I learned and grew each day.

But the commute. Three hours a day, four types of transportation, hundreds of steps and twelve hours away from home. I'd done it for over twenty years, but severe arthritis made it harder every day.

I knew God's answer to my question, and finally ended my career at Christmas.

I tried not to growl when people said, "Congratulations."

Floundering, I stumbled through figuring out this new life. I established routines to be accomplished every day. I joined a small Bible study group and volunteered to do some cooking at church. I looked for new purpose, and I struggled with loneliness.

On the horizon, I became aware of a small, black cloud — people in China were falling ill and dying in alarming numbers. I knew a family in China so I prayed for their safety. Then I talked to God about the important things, like my crushing loneliness and what should I be doing with my time.

In March, that tiny cloud grew and spread over the sky outside my house. The Prime Minister said school would close for an extra two weeks for March break. Then students began learning online. Now we wondered about September. At church they showed us how to hip bump rather than hug, which I privately thought silly. I hugged anyway. Then the building closed and all services occurred online.

It got worse. I made the gritted-teeth admission that I had entered the age bracket of *senior* and had to grocery shop with them at 7 A.M. When I brought my groceries home, I washed and disinfected them. I bought my first mask. I washed and washed and washed my hands.

"You thought you were lonely?" I mused. "You had no idea. I forsee new depths of lonely ahead which you are about to experience."

A new granddaughter arrived. Sweet and plump with a head full of dark hair. At least, that's what I can see from her pictures. I haven't held her yet, or played with her sisters for months.

Six weeks later, another granddaughter arrived. I offered long-distance support and encouragement for nursing problems and other family difficulties.

Just when it couldn't get any worse, it did.

Nineteen positive cases in my former workplace turned it into a war zone. The homey atmosphere evaporated as residents ate in their rooms and pictures of staff showed them wearing masks, gowns and gloves as if they'd just left an operating room. I thanked God I'd listened and left when I did, but I mourned for those I loved. Then my mourning became more real as five of my beloved ladies died.

Alone on my couch, I cried. "God, You are still God. You are still in charge, and You still love me. What would you like me to do?"

In the silence of my living room, I heard His voice whisper, "Encourage."

I looked for ways to encourage myself. I walked each day and took photographs of a world emerging from winter. I looked for beauty and saw it everywhere. I posted my photos online to encourage others.

I saw my prayer time as more than going through my list, but an opportunity to help others by lifting them up to the Father. As I prayed for my children and grandchildren each day, I asked God for new and creative ways to connect with them.

My walks became opportunities to reach out to neighbors. I gave the kids next door some sidewalk chalk I had in the garage, and the little girl wrote "best neighbour" on the end of my driveway. I chatted with a lady down the street at a safe distance, and caught up with a couple who used to live in my townhouse complex as we passed on the pathway. Each contact felt like a gift.

I found new and creative ways to celebrate. A parade of cars, a birthday breakfast delivered, sending paper airplanes with messages of love for the retirement of an airline employee. I began to realize that celebrations could be different and still wonderful. Maybe more so.

I found ways to give. Special grocery shopping for the food bank. Sewing masks for the staff at work to wear as they travel in transit. Cookies for the kids next door.

It's June 3, 2020 and we still live in isolation. My community tried to slowly open a few businesses but cases spiked so caution prevails. I'm still lonely and my grandma's arms still ache for time with my girls. I desperately need a haircut and a pedicure. I'll never take a hug for granted again.

But each day, I ask God how He wants to use me.

And He answers.

For now, that's enough.

11

Our Only True Stabilizer

Sherry Diane Kitts

The bedroom shook as a commotion jarred us from sleep one morning in January. My husband ran to the patio door to find out what was going on.

"Come look at this," he said. "They're taking down the trees."

I looked over his shoulder, dumbfounded by the scene unfolding before us.

"What's happening?"

The tree-filled lot behind our home buzzed with humming motors, beeping trucks, colliding metal, and crashing trees.

"I guess they sold the lot, and they're clearing it to build a house."

We'd lived in a quiet neighborhood for twenty years and enjoyed the little forest in the lot behind our home. But it disappeared from our sight within a few hours.

Houses emerged around us as more lots were cleared over the next several weeks. We'd grown accustomed to the rural setting and privacy it afforded, and wanted to voice our objections. The choice wasn't ours to make, however, and we had no control over the development in progress.

In the months to come, more changes occurred, but with a greater magnitude. However, these changes didn't awaken us in the morning with loud noises; they caught us off guard like an experienced pickpocket.

We were attacked without warning, as a deadly virus swept across America.

The president ordered a nation-wide quarantine, and we all learned new guidelines for living.

Stores, schools, travel, events, restaurants, and places of employment shut their doors to the public, and we isolated ourselves from family and friends.

COVID-19 changed our world. Our customary way of life ground to a halt. Once again, we found ourselves with no choice as the virus' claws tightened around us.

The residential construction continued in our neighborhood during our remaining quarantine at home. It was good to see some people still able to work, and their circus-like operations entertained us. Elephant-sized trucks lugged down our street heavy with dirt and block. Hippo-like drums on the cement trucks rolled around with a mixture of sand and water. Acrobatic men balanced themselves on perpendicular rooftops. Yellow giraffe-necked cranes ambled onto the lots lifting loads impossible for humans. Electric nail guns pop, pop, popped along with tunes blasting from the radio. It was impressive.

One afternoon, I watched as an operator maneuvered a crane across the sandy soil. Trucks had left ruts and holes around the lot where it needed to be positioned. I wondered if the operator was aware of the uneven ground. How would he steady the machinery on such terrain? However, the man didn't seem surprised by the conditions because he never hesitated. Instead, he unfolded the outriggers horizontally from the chassis and moved them vertically to level and stabilize the crane. Although the danger was obvious, the operator handled the crane with precision, and lifted the roof trusses with the finesse of a seasoned performer.

We all need a Master Operator. Life as we know it can suddenly cease when our security crumbles around us. However, God understands the operation of everything, and knows how to accurately guide our every move. He is our security and can help us overcome human limitations.

Although our world has been shaken, the Lord God can balance us, steady us, and sustain us through the rough terrain. In Psalm 62 the psalmist, David, talks about finding rest and hope in God. He compares God to a rock and a fortress in Whom we can trust.

Our Creator and Father God provides the surety of sustenance for all situations and strong footing on uneven grounds. Like the crane's outriggers, His arms reach out to save and stabilize us. The circus of life can shake us and rearrange our landscape, but God can handle our load. As our only true stabilizer, He can balance us securely onto a level plane of peace.

Thank you, Father God, for being our refuge and our constant guide and support. Thank you for stabilizing our foundations in treacherous times.

12

Connecting Through Isolation

Fran Braga Meininger

I anticipated the proclamation and felt sure the order to shelter in place would continue another month. I suspected it might be even longer.

As I sat gazing out at the fading evening light, watching another day turn to night, I realized I had already lost count. I distracted myself with thoughts of how I would occupy my time, what projects to undertake, how to spend the empty hours doing something meaningful. I wasn't overly concerned. It is my nature to be productive.

But there was something else amiss, an unsettling, unnerving sensation that rumbled within. And as I inhaled a long-measured breath, it rose up, a longing, not for activity or distraction, but for connection. I knew its emotion. I am only too familiar with it, having met up many time throughout the years when I drifted too far afield and lost touch with those I need to be whole, or when I shuttered myself off out of frustration or fear.

I drifted off to sleep that night contemplating how human connection could be sustained through this unprecedented time of isolation. Intentional as it was, it didn't make the result any more tolerable. How would I satisfy my need, how would I broach the topic of it without feeling embarrassed? How would I touch another while sustaining the safety of social distancing?

Human connection is as basic to me as my need for air and water. It is essential to my well-being. I thrive when the connection is vibrant and wither along with it when it shrivels and shrinks away. I know from experience the answer lies in reaching out beyond the insecurity, with candor and intimacy. I have to abandon the safeguards that normally protect me from being nicked by rejection and speak my truth, admit my trepidation and ask to have my needs met, in plain and open effort.

Now is a time to be vulnerable, to accept that I am, and let it show through. We all are, no matter how strong and self-assured, or how reluctant we are to own it. This global catastrophe is bigger than our collective bravado and it is weighing on us. It is a monster that lurks under the bed in the silent darkness and whispers its threats when we are most defenseless. Without the reassurance of human contact, it may convince us we are alone to fend for ourselves.

It doesn't have to be that way. I know the isolation of an anxious mind. I've lived with it most of my life, but I've learned over the years how to step over the fear and shame of my emotions, and I will do so now.

I have to reach out however possible, ask for company when I need it, invite others to share six foot distanced walks, fill the long, vacant hours with the companionship of someone I know cares. I have to ask for what I need and want, not expect it to be divined in some magical way, as I sit here guarded and expecting. I am not alone, and these feelings are not exclusively mine. I've learned when I speak up, and express what lies behind my façade, I spark a reaction in others who, like me, may be waiting for someone to be the first to reach out. I have to be the first.

There is a bond that forms as eyes meet, it goes beyond words, to what lies behind them. I will be with those who feel comfortable with a personal encounter at an acceptable distance, and will use other means to connect with my friends who prefer FaceTime and video. Technology may be a less personal approach to human contact, but it does allow me to see for myself how those I love are faring. I will speak honestly and openly about how I am doing, and ask of others to share with me how they are and what I can do to comfort them. I will reach out, be kind, listen deeply and to understand, and I will offer love.

This is a time to live cautiously and protect our health, but it is not a time to be cautious with our hearts.

13
Contentment as Power

Karen Cook

The COVID-19 pandemic was different for me than many people I knew. My friends' and neighbors' lives came to an abrupt stop while my life continued much as before. At the beginning of the breakout I worked at a bank. I was an essential worker, so I went to work as normal.

On my breaks or after work I would check in via social media with my quarantined friends. They were making the most of the time off. They painted walls, took on-line classes, Zoom-chatted with relatives.

Watching the posts about lives slowing down and seeing quarantine survival tips gave me the herd feeling as if I had more leisure time for myself. So I'd get home from work and pull out my list of projects — and get exhausted and overwhelmed. It took me a while to realize that I was forty hours short of the free time my quarantine friends were enjoying.

My bank job became a casualty of the virus. I had about a week to mourn and enjoy the Shelter-in-Place order before I, fortunately, found another job. During that week, I planted seeds for a garden, deleted old emails, baked bread, played games with my teenagers, completed a puzzle, and went for early-morning walks. I thought, "So this is what everyone is doing?" Then my taste of the stay-at-home window closed and I went back to work.

I feel like there has been a national rest going on. People have rediscovered their homes and families and cherished their friends. Unlike most people, I didn't get the chance to rest; my life's pace never slowed down. I still put a lunch together, hurry to work and come home to crash. Life seems very normal that way.

Some things are not normal, of course. My daughter's high school graduation became a non-event. Happily, she has the continual comfort of her younger sister. It was nice to have them home at all times, laughing and staying up all night talking. Different, but not a bad thing.

I am sure that the COVID crisis will seem unreal to me as I look back on it years from now. As if it's something everyone else went through. I'll remember my normal current of life's rhythm flowing past the dammed up pools of my friend's lives. But my unusual path through COVID gave me some solid life lessons.

I think this is the main one I've taken to heart. I hear this verse quoted a lot: *I can do all this through him who gives me strength* (Philippians 4:13). Many times the intent of the quote gives the idea that God can help us power through anything — like a global pandemic.

But in the preceding verses Paul, writing this from a prison cell, hints at a prerequisite for that power: *I am not saying this because I am in need, for I have learned to be content whatever the circumstances. I know what it is to be in need, and I know what it is to have plenty. I have learned the secret of being content in any and every situation, whether well fed or hungry, whether living in plenty or in want"* (Philippians 4:11-12).

Paul learned from his life's joys and woes to stay in a place of contentment. His secret to tapping into God's power was to keep a heavenly perspective. And this was not an automatic thing. He learned. The original Greek says he was taught and instructed.

In many ways, COVID taught me that, though I did not suffer as much as others, I did need the lesson of learning to be content. I did not get the rest I felt others had, but I abounded in the fact I *could* work.

I could just as easily been out of work.

I could have been disturbed by the daily death totals on the news.

I could have mourned the dissolved plans for my daughter's graduation party.

I could have blasted Facebook with political jabs over governmental decisions.

I could have found a hundred reasons to be upset, but God was teaching me to be content — even though my friends were making homemade laundry soap and painting their bathrooms or playing board games with their kids each night.

This crisis is unique, but not the last. Like Paul, we need to allow God to work His mighty strength through our practice of contentment.

14

Don't Give in to Fear

Stephanie Pavlantos

*God hath not given us the spirit of fear;
but of power, and of love, and of a sound mind.*
~ 2 Timothy 1:7 KJV

I like the King James Version of this verse because it uses the phrase "sound mind" instead of self-discipline or self-control. Fear tends to make us conjure up a lot of possible (usually frightening) outcomes as a response to something we can't control.

I am not usually a fearful person, but this past week tested me.

My twenty-three-year-old daughter started showing symptoms of the coronavirus on Tuesday — sore throat, headache, and fever. We hoped it was a normal virus or cold. But by Friday, she had pressure in her chest and was weak and dizzy.

She could barely walk across the room without resting. She was nauseated if she thought about eating.

My momma heart hurt for her, and fear was crouching at the door of my emotions. I told the Lord I didn't want to give in to the fear threatening to overtake me. I told Him this many times. I kept praying for Alexandria.

I have twins who were preemies — born at twenty-seven weeks. They had their share of ventilators, pneumonia, and asthma. We worried Alexandria's lungs could be ripe for this virus.

Let me just say here she was never officially tested or diagnosed. We were told to stay away from hospitals and doctors' offices unless she was having trouble breathing. She wasn't. So we stayed away.

We have a holistic approach to health care. So, we had her on liquid silver and zinc, and vitamins A, B, C, and D. I felt like a pill pusher.

On Friday morning, my husband and I anointed her and prayed for healing. During prayer, the Lord gave me a picture of Alexandria as an infant in the NICU isolate. I remembered that day.

We received a call at 4:30 A.M. telling us our baby girl was in critical condition. She had pneumonia in both lungs. She was no longer breathing on her own.

When I arrived at the NICU, my extremely sick baby girl was gray and still. The doctor had given her a drug to paralyze her so she would not fight the ventilator. We prayed for her and asked everyone we knew to pray for healing.

So, as I saw this picture in my mind, I felt as though the Lord reminded me that He healed her then and He could heal her now.

Peace ran through my body, just as it had twenty-three years ago.

Monday morning Alexandria got up, feeling like herself again. The fever was gone, the headache, aches and pains disappeared. She wanted to eat.

I am thankful for all the people who were praying for our daughter. But, mostly, I am thankful for my Heavenly Father who knew her plight and never left her or our family.

My family was in quarantine for two weeks. The rest of us had no symptoms of the virus. But my house seemed small with five adults here. All. Day. Long!

I am thankful for friends who dropped off groceries . . . and hair color, too.

We have much to be thankful for. We have homes, food, and people who love and care for us.

We didn't give in to fear. It had and has no place in our home or life. Give it to Jesus and let Him send it back to the place it came from.

15

Strange Season, Unique Gifts

Lauren Craft

A tall fence divided us. Squinting through the sunlight, I could see about a dozen seniors who had gathered on the back patio of their nursing home. Our group of six volunteers from the local Baptist church stood beyond the tall fence posts, setting up a microphone and instruments.

The staff had explained that the residents had been starved for companionship in this strange season of isolation. No visitors were allowed inside and none of the residents could leave the complex. This was necessary of course to protect the elderly from COVID-19, but it left a void in their hearts. Bible study groups and pastors hadn't been coming by for fellowship anymore, and friends and family could no longer visit.

Reaching out to needy people was difficult during the pandemic, but it was needed more than ever before. Our church members wanted desperately to make a difference.

When the center invited us to host a fellowship time of stories and songs beyond the back patio, I was thrilled, but apprehension tightened my stomach. I'd need a lot of help and creativity to make something like this work.

Organizing nursing home visits had been easy before the coronavirus pandemic, but this would be tricky. *Would the residents be able to hear us? Could we make a connection, even though we couldn't hug the elders and kiss their foreheads like before?* I had so many questions. More than ever, I needed the body of Christ to come together, pooling together the distinct gifts and talents found within our church family.

My first call was to my friend Gabi, a multimedia expert on staff at our church. "Which microphone should I buy?" I asked. "Does this one hook into a speaker? Will that plug into that?"

The options were so confusing. Online orders took longer during the pandemic, and I had no time to waste with silly mistakes. I knew I would buy the wrong thing without her guidance.

She recommended a system and sent me the link. The mic and speaker arrived the day before the fellowship. *This is it*, I thought as I tore open the box in the middle of my foyer. *If it doesn't work, we'll either have to scream our lungs out or cancel the fellowship.* But I knew God wouldn't have brought us this far — and given me a knowledgeable helper — only to let everything topple to the ground.

I tested it. When my voice boomed and echoed off the walls of my entryway, I breathed a deep gulp of relief. Gabi had averted a disaster.

Then the big day arrived. That afternoon, the six of us made our way to the back of the building just beyond the gate.

Children volunteers are always a highlight for the elderly, and this visit was no exception. Holding the microphone, a girl named Hannah shared the story of Jesus walking on water. In the story, Peter joined Jesus on the sea but began to sink when the winds and waves hastened, until Jesus pulled him up.

After reading, Hannah shared the meaning behind the passage: keeping our eyes on Jesus even during the storms of life. A reminder we all — including me — needed during the storm caused by COVID-19 and the economic downturn.

Two volunteers, Ed and Daniel, played songs on the violin and the harmonica. Some were old and dear to me, like "Amazing Grace," and some were fresh and new, including "This Is My Father's World." Their talent, hard work, and practice showed. The songs brought smiles to the faces of the seniors, and what mattered most was that they were using their skills for such a good purpose.

Ed also shared a Bible message from Ecclesiastes Chapter 3 on the many seasons of life, another passage that sank deep into our hearts because of the strange season in which we lived. An elderly man was touched by the message and later spoke to Ed about it through the fence posts. As we left, Ed carried the speaker to my car. It is always helpful to have an "Ed" around.

The opportunities didn't end with the back patio fellowship. We have many crafty people in our congregation who made encouragement cards for the seniors.

We decided on "bear hugs" as our theme, and of course, each person came up with different, brilliant ideas. My friend, Stef, drew small bears with the message, "This bear cares for you." A teen student, Hailey, made a card with a polar bear wearing a tie. Another student, Claire, drew a bear with a honey pot on one of her creations. My heart leapt when I saw the products of their imagination and handiwork.

The nursing home also gave us the opportunity to make encouragement posters for their hard-working staff. My first thought was that I could simply print out messages and glue them on poster board, but then I thought again. My friend Basma, who attends my church and lives right next door, is a gifted artist who would do a much better job. To get her going, I typed and printed basic thank you messages for the center of each poster — one for the cooks, one for the nurses, and so on — but left plenty of space for Basma to add decorations.

When she showed me the finished, decorated signs a few days later, I stood speechless in the grassy patch between our houses. She had drawn a collage of handmade images for each group of employees. For the housekeepers, for example, she had drawn images — incredibly *life-like* images — of things like yellow kitchen gloves, cleaning spray, and a sponge. For the servers, she had drawn a pie and a roast chicken that made me want to grab a plate and dig in. For the nurses, she drew a stethoscope, a blood pressure machine, and used a real Band-aid as a sticker. Each poster was more exceptional than the last. I could tell she had spent hours upon hours on each.

Scripture tells us *there are different kinds of gifts, but the same Spirit distributes them. There are different kinds of service, but the same Lord. There are different kinds of working, but in all of them and in everyone it is the same God at work* 1 Corinthians 12:4-6.

The unique efforts of my brothers and sisters in Christ were making the truth of that passage come to life.

Eventually I found the words to thank Basma, even though they fell short.

"This is unbelievable. It will make such an impact because of the thought you put into it. My just printing and gluing words wouldn't have been as meaningful at all," I said.

"Yes, but look at what you wrote," my friend said, pointing to the different messages I had written. "They're so good. I wouldn't have known what to write."

I blushed at her compliment. I had been so amazed at the gifts of others that I hadn't realized my own contribution.

Maybe *you* can write. Maybe you can lift things. Maybe you can draw pictures, play an instrument, or prevent a technical disaster.

Whatever our gifts are, God will use them powerfully. Even in the strangest of seasons.

16
A Dark and Stormy Night in Quarantine

Terri R. Miller

A string of clear, unseasonably cool spring evenings was brought to an abrupt end in our little Southeast Alabama town on a Thursday evening in late April, 2020 when a massive storm front moved through. Though the weather had been fair earlier in the day, the thunder that rumbled in the distance in the late afternoon warned of the storm's imminent approach. A gathering of ominous dark clouds blocked out the sun, causing the day to look as if night had come.

I had already been on the edge of lunacy from weeks of being locked away in a hateful quarantine from friends and family, including a newborn granddaughter. The quarantine was imposed in an effort to control the spread of the coronavirus, better known as COVID-19. The only reprieve had been the beautiful spring weather which allowed me to get outside the four walls of the house and breathe in some freedom. Sitting outside in the evenings around the firepit had become a ritual I looked forward to as each day drew to a close. I relished pulling my bulky sweater cozily around me against the crisp night air. The reality of the virus had seemed very far away as I stoked the fire and gazed up into the diamond-studded sky above me.

On this night I wasn't allowed that escape as cool air and warm air violently collided. My nerves were on edge as I sat and listened to the howling wind and pounding rain. It had only been a little over a year since a devastating tornado had ripped through our community, and the memory of its destruction had me struggling to push aside rising panic.

While I stood at the kitchen window watching the lightening streak across the sky, I stewed over the feeling of being trapped inside after a long day of working from my home office. Despite the cup of warm chamomile tea I sipped, my mood grew darker with each passing moment. The nightly excursion into my own backyard had become a welcome distraction from thoughts of the virus and the sad state of the world in general. Without that diversion, I was left to wander around in my own mind.

Just when I'd angrily resigned myself to settling in and searching for a movie to watch, a clap of thunder boomed so loudly that it literally rattled the china in the cabinets and caused me to jump so violently that I sloshed the tea out of my cup and onto my shirt. The lights flickered and went out, taking the internet with them. There I stood, in the dark with tea on my shirt and not even Netflix to distract me from my self-pity. Except for the sounds of the storm, there was silence. The air around me felt thick and invasive, pressing down on me until I was sure I would be crushed.

I felt my way to the kitchen counter, set my cup down, and fumbled for a towel to wipe up the spilt tea. With every second that passed, my breathing grew quicker and heavier. The pounding of my heart in my ears was drowning out the sound of the storm.

This was just too much to bear. For more than a month now, I had been denied the fellowship of family and friends, the ability to attend church, the luxury of a haircut, privilege of toilet paper on the store shelves, and now the one thing I'd found pleasure in and that had kept me sane through all of this was being snatched away.

It was all so unfair. Why was this happening? Was God allowing this? Couldn't He just make it all go away? I pounded my fist on the counter and spat out the angry words, "What in the world are you trying to say, God?"

The words echoed back and forth trapped in the room by the enveloping blackness.

"What in the world . . . in the world . . . in the world."

They swirled round and round coaxing and stirring.

"In the world . . . in the world. . . ."

I felt a shift as the rhythm of the echo pulled at a well, hidden deep inside me.

"In the world . . . in the world. . . ."

From the well, the truth of a Bible verse sprang up.

In the world you will have trouble but be of good cheer. I have overcome the world. (John 16:33 NIV)

The raging, discontented voices fell silent. I exhaled deeply not even aware that I had been holding my breath. A calm settled over me displacing the worry and fear that had plagued me for weeks. The words were embracing me.

Tears welled up. Not tears of anger or sorrow, but tears of joy and relief. This was the answer I was longing for. A reminder that God is greater than anything I face. Everything that comes against me has already been defeated. Every virus, every storm, every fear. All have been conquered at the cross of Jesus.

I breathed a prayer of thanksgiving.

Thankful for the roof over my head that was sheltering me from the storm.

Thankful for my family and friends.

Thankful for a loving, faithful God who never leaves me.

The storm outside continued to rage, but the storm inside had been stilled with just a word from the Master of the storm.

17
Praying Through the Darkness

L. C. Helms

Because I am immune compromised, any sickness I have can last for weeks, or longer. I've always feared getting the flu, a cold, or virus. So it's understandable that documentaries on the next Big Pandemic caught my eye. And then right out of a dystopian thriller, here came the COVID-19 virus.

My brother and I were on a ten-day cruise in the Caribbean before I was opening a private counseling practice. I planned to finish setting things up when I got home. Everything was going great. I'd found my new office, was enjoying a long-anticipated trip with my brother, and had twelve days to do nothing but laugh and relax.

When news about two cruise ships and a virus blared from the cabin television, I couldn't believe it. I'd been on a cruise when the Norwalk virus broke out, and that had gone disastrously downhill. Now I felt bad for the passengers on the two ill-fated ships but I was sure we would be fine. It was impossible the virus would be onboard our ship, too . . . or make it to the United States.

Then unusual things began to occur on board. Sanitizing became mandatory. We couldn't serve ourselves at meals, and something strange began happening in port: Crew members were being checked and taken off ship.

People on board were now getting sick. One person died on board.

No one talked about it. Then someone else died. We were not told how, why, or what anyone had. During the last few days of the cruise, I was praying we would not be quarantined or stranded.

Once home, I set up my office and went back to life as usual. I'd just transitioned to a new church, joined the Sunday School class, and introduced my grandchildren to the Wednesday night kids group.

But then the virus arrived, we were quarantined, and everything shut down completely, including my office.

I was alone. My daughter threatened me if I left the house. I have a large yard so I wasn't too bothered at first. I enjoy quiet spaces, down time at home.

My uncle and I remained in a strong pen-pal relationship. My aunt had died over the summer and he was still experiencing grief. His letters shared with me the terrible things happening in Maine due to the virus. I watched the news constantly and kept tabs on the number of people dying. But as my anxiety increased I realized I had to set limits on how much news I watched.

Afraid to go to the store, I lived off whatever was in my pantry and became quite creative with leftovers. I began to bake all kinds of bread and anything else I could generate from my storehouse of uneaten pantry items. During the first week of the stay-at-home order my freezer quit working so I phoned the local appliance store. They told me the store had only two freezers left and they'd be sold out by 5 p.m. . . . and they weren't able to get any more. I was shocked, but of course I bought one sight unseen; I needed a freezer. Soon everyone in town was sold out of freezers as well . . . along with toilet paper, paper towels, sanitizer, and bread yeast.

Suddenly I wanted a puppy but the breed I wanted was unavailable. "It's the COVID-19," the dozens of people I called told me. "Everyone wants a companion dog and all the breeders have sold everything they have and have already taken orders on the next litters.

Disheartened, I stayed busy writing, reading, and baking bread.

On Easter I took a drive-thru take-out for two to my mother's home where we sat ten feet apart and enjoyed each other's company for an hour.

My cousin, a pastor in Maine, began to do his messages through YouTube, and I was able to watch them. It was wonderful to feel like I was there. I watched many church services like his; they were now everywhere on the Internet.

When my brother decided we should all have a Zoom Bible study I was all in. He also suggested we set aside a special time to pray each day. This began my journey into intercessory prayer. I'd spent my life wanting to pray like a warrior. I'd watched others pray and get results. Now it was my turn. No more procrastination. I had to be accountable to everyone in the study. And so I prayed.

At first, my prayers were small, difficult, and awkward: prayers for the study, for family, for myself. Then I began to roam through the house praying, interceding for lost family and friends, praying for the sick, the elderly, the broken. I was learning how wonderful time alone with God can be. My fear of catching the virus and dying disappeared, but I remained home at the request of my children.

Surprisingly, prospective clients began to call for counseling appointments. The governor had mandated that counselors not see clients in person, but the order was confusing, so I phoned the governor's office to get clarification. Each time I called I had to leave a message. No one ever called back.

I'd never seen a client virtually before and was scared to death. The clients refused to wait until COVID-19 was gone, however, so I began to see new clients online through telehealth. My practice began to grow.

I quickly realized anxiety levels were increasing. Isolation was getting to people. They wanted human interaction, connection, church services, and friends. The world was changing very fast and no one seemed prepared to handle it.

I was one person. I kept praying.

A counselor friend called. She said she had gone to the emergency room and they refused to test her but ruled out everything else and told her she had COVID. She had self-quarantined before it was mandatory yet she still got the virus. Now she was extremely sick. She was middle-aged and although she had a cough, and a terrible headache, she said she was managing. We kept in touch daily. I had seltzer water and zinc sent to her home. I prayed. Her fever spiked to 104 for days. Her headache became excruciating. The nightmares were horrid. One night at 10:00 she told me she smelled of death, and thought she was going to die. For no one to be able to go to my friend, to hold her, to look into her eyes and comfort her was a victory for this terrible virus.

She recovered, but she says even now something has happened to her brain. She forgets and it takes time for her to think of things, to sort them out. She's sad and cries a lot more now.

*

After the stay-at-home order was lifted I began seeing my daughter's family. Then my daughter and her husband told me they'd both tested positive for COVID-19, and the doctor explained the likelihood that my two grandchildren were also infected.

One night about a week later I thought I was developing symptoms. I couldn't concentrate on the movie I was watching and I kept coughing. There was a strange coldness deep in my chest that I couldn't explain. Then I woke up in the middle of the night with severe pain in my back and under my shoulder blade. I jumped out of bed to move around until the pain went away.

I soon panicked and within minutes couldn't breathe. In my panic I realized I didn't have a Will. *What if I end up in the hospital or I die during this pandemic?* I ran into my study and typed out my last will and testament, and then began to pray. I was sure COVID couldn't possibly come on so quickly, though, and I realized just how fearful I was. I gave God the fear and kept praying until I was indeed ready to meet my maker.

That night, I came to personally understand what fear can do, and how prayer can quench fear's devastating effects.

As yet, I haven't gotten COVID, or had another panic attack.

And although I didn't get a puppy, I now have a six-year-old rescue dog that is a lot of company. The long days being stuck at home don't seem as long with her around.

Although I love being alone, and thrive in seclusion, I realize strange things happen when we isolate ourselves from each other for too long. People need people. We need to feel someone's gentle touch. The way their lips curve into an encouraging smile. I find myself wanting to connect with others more than I ever had before, and I appreciate church more than ever.

I did begin to see clients in person again. And after nearly three months I went shopping for the first time. It felt good to be in a store, to feel human, to connect. It also felt odd when guards manned the doors and allowed only so many to enter the store at a time.

Although I hate wearing a mask, I keep one in my purse now for fear I'll forget it at home, and someone will be angry and yell at me for not helping keep them safe from a virus I might possibly be carrying.

I feel like I'm in a different country and the world is not the same place anymore.

So I just keep praying. The knowledge that God has everything under control sustains me and gives me strength. In my heart a peace that passes understanding reminds me that I am His, and He is mine. And I know that I am ready to meet Him face to face.

18

Staying Home

Loretta Eidson

My husband, Ken, and I arrived for our first day at the training center to learn how to administer his dialysis treatments in our home. Since I'm not a nurse, and never worked in the medical field, this training had me apprehensive and nervous about home therapy.

A nurse met us at the door of the clinic, took our temperatures, gave us each a mask, and squirted sanitizer on our hands. She escorted us to a small room where we'd spend eight hours a day for the next twelve days learning how to handle wound care, catheter site care, tubing, and dialysis solutions.

If we touched anything but the supplies, we had to rewash our hands with antibacterial soap for two minutes using a timer, dry them with paper towels, then apply sanitizer. This process went on multiple times each session. The purpose was to help us perfect the sterilization process before handling dialysis equipment. Trust me; our hands had never been so clean.

My biggest issue was the mask. The only mask I'd ever worn was a silly one at a Fall Festival, but I'd worn that only a short time. When COVID-19 hit, wearing a mask became a daily requirement across the nation. Instead of being suspicious of "the masked man," we became concerned with those who didn't wear one.

Breathing my own breath behind that little blue medical facemask felt suffocating. I slid it down under my nose on multiple occasions and took a few freeing breaths before putting it back in place. I was relieved when each day's training ended. As soon as I walked out the door, the mask came off, and I stuffed it into my purse.

Then the governor announced a stay-at-home order. Stores closed, doctors' offices shifted to virtual video appointments, hospitals took patients but didn't allow family or friends to visit. Grocery store shelves rapidly emptied, leaving patrons scrambling for necessities. Because of this order, police and the national guard blocked the main roads, checking to see if we were considered *essential* workers. For them, essential meant anyone in the medical field, drug store employees, grocery store workers, or city employees, which included the police department and fire department.

This stay-at-home order wasn't an option for us. We were among the *essential*. Ken's health required him to have dialysis daily, which meant we had to go to the clinic every day until we'd completed the training and had the equipment to do dialysis at home. When we completed the last day of training, I danced in the parking lot. We could go home and stay, as the governor ordered — no more long days of classes.

While some people were unhappy about being required to stay home, Ken and I found we were thrilled. Our days at the clinic had been long, tense, and tiring. Home was where we wanted to be.

At home, we celebrated our success by cooking cheeseburgers on the grill in our backyard. Had that been a typical day, we would have celebrated at our favorite steakhouse, but the restaurants were closed due to COVID-19 and the stay-at-home order.

"I'm going to work in the flower beds," Ken said as he traipsed out the door.

"Great. I'm going into my office and catch up on some writing commitments."

I stood in the doorway of my office and let out a peaceful sigh. "Yes, finally, I can get back to my keyboard." And that I did.

The days slipped by without a worry. We enjoyed our morning coffee together and watched the starlings soar around the birdhouse from our dining room's bay window. A hummingbird made its appearance a few times while red, gray, and yellow finches stood their ground around the hummingbird feeders.

After coffee, Ken worked his magic on the lawn and planted more flowers. His green thumb can grow just about anything. He loves the outdoors and is perfectly happy staying home. I even found the time to assist with cutting the grass.

My office welcomed me as I settled in and wrote a few stories for anthologies, worked on my newsletter, updated my website, finished a manuscript, and started another novel. During this time, publishers accepted three of my six short stories for publication.

The introvert in me delighted at the opportunity to stay home and write to my heart's content.

I began cooking again — aomething I'd drifted away from over the years of writing. I'd opted for the fast food carry-out options rather than home-cooked meals, but the stay-at-home order forced me to re-ignite my love for grilling, and for healthier choices.

We missed our family, but with face-time and Zoom, we had many opportunities to see each other and catch up on family happenings. My daughter, Tracy, was my grocery-shopping buddy. She and I wore gloves and masks while we shopped at our local Walmart. As soon as we made it back to the car, we shed the masks and the gloves and doused our hands with sanitizer.

My son, Carey, showed up on our doorstep on many occasions to fix my computer and settings on our television. Hand sanitizer made its way around the room as we celebrated our technically-minded son. Of course, I fed him dinner, too.

The absolute funniest — well, the weirdest — thing that happened to me during the COVID-19 stay-at-home order was during a shopping spree at Walmart. I rose early one Tuesday morning and raced to the store during their 6:00-7:00 A.M. Senior Hour. Since hand sanitizer, antibacterial soap, hydrogen peroxide, toilet paper, and paper towels had become rare during this time, I made a beeline to hunt for those supplies.

I was thrilled to grab the last sixty-four-ounce bottle of Dial antibacterial liquid soap, along with a thirty-two-ounce bottle of hydrogen peroxide, and a twelve-pack of Bounty paper towels. I held my head high, pleased that my trip was worth losing another hour of sleep.

Happily, I went to the meat counter for a package of ground beef. I turned my back on my basket long enough to decide which package of meat I wanted. When I turned around, my happiness quickly fizzled. Someone had taken items from my basket. My treasures were gone!

What?

A worker in the meat department stopped when he saw me with my hands in the air, and my mouth wide open in surprise. "Can I help you?" he asked.

"Someone took items from my basket when I wasn't looking."

He raised an eyebrow. "Are you sure that's your basket?"

Of course it was my basket. I wondered how many seniors could run fast enough to swipe my treasures and get away without being seen. By the time I returned home, I had to laugh at the scene I had envisioned of a little old lady grabbing the items, tucking them under her arm, and scurrying away as fast as she could to put distance between us. Lord love her, she must have needed them more than I did.

I am saddened that COVID-19 has caused such devastation in our nation and so many have lost their lives. My heart goes out to them and their families. But here, in my personal space, the stay-at-home order forced me to push the reset button on my way of thinking about daily living, family, and my relationship with Christ.

My prayer is that others will rediscover the value of life, find peace in the midst of chaos, and experience a renewed faith in Jesus Christ.

19
My Pandemic Play

Joanne DiRienzo Schloeman

All the world's a stage, and all the men and women merely players.

Shakespeare

When the change in all our lives was unfolding, as stores closed and services diminished, as events were cancelled, lives disappeared and the media fed our fears, thoughts of agitation and panic crept into my life. I had never thought I would experience a pandemic in my lifetime. I was surprised by the unfamiliar character developing within me and desperately wanted to seek refuge. Another part of my character, more familiar to me, reminded me to be outwardly focused and to bring comfort to those who were suffering, just in the way I receive comfort from God. What would my part on this world's stage be?

I turned to my Savior first for comfort and then to experts, leaders, and the media for guidance. I was under the impression that a person can find comfort in manuals, handbooks, reference guides, or thick packets of procedures, by relying on them in order to feel secure and prepared in the event of a pandemic.

Faced with this crisis, I found I could choose to react to the event or choose to be proactive to cope with the event.

I gathered stamps, cards, envelopes, Bible passages and a list of phone numbers. My hands shuffled through the materials, preparing my act of compassion to those I knew needed hope and comfort. I reflected on how my life orbits around my family, my church, and my God.

Meditating on my church and all the countries that have altered their way of life during this critical time, my mind nudged me to my past. Living a few hours outside of New York, I have experienced many Broadway plays. To the audience, these plays and musicals appeared flawless. A successful stage presence is vital to delivering unwrinkled performances. The cast, production crew and all who are involved in the production are what create this magical experience.

I wondered how my own "Pandemic Play" would unfold. Would it be a play of terror, fear, and suspense, or one of hope and love for others? Would I be a box office expert navigating through the process in a confident, business-like fashion, or would fear and uncertainty cause me to scatter seeds of despair, hopelessness, and gloom? How would I portray my character? Would I choose to be proactive or become paralyzed by fear?

We are all actors on the stage and each play a part in this thing called "life." We have been challenged during this time, weaving together a way to adapt to the circumstances, either inwardly or outwardly focused.

When a play comes to a close, the massive dark red satin curtain is drawn down to let the audience know that the play has ended. The cast members dash back on stage one at a time smiling ear to ear, and are recognized by the audience. Cheers and applause sound throughout theatre. There is always a main character in the play. This person appears at the very end of the cast introduction and receives shouts of acclamation, bravos, and a standing ovation.

Today and always, our Savior Jesus is the star of the show. He is our Redeemer, and, as the hymn says, "because He lives we can face tomorrow." With all of the closures, cancellations and loss of life, I am reminded that God's work is never cancelled! Our Savior is the one who receives the standing ovation. He is the reference guide to our pandemic protocol. Without Him the pages remain blank. In a life of choices, He is our ticket to a forever "open" and an everlasting future with Him.

20

Trust God Even During a Pandemic

Evelyn Mann

Being a big news buff, I read reports of China experiencing a novel coronavirus in January 2020. It never occurred to me we'd experience the effects of this contagious virus from halfway around the world in our small suburb of Tampa, Florida. As mom of a special-needs child, my motivation in following this story was inspired by our little miracle, Samuel.

In 2005, I gave birth to our son who has a rare form of dwarfism called Thanatophoric Dwarfism. Considering "Thanatophoric" in Greek means heaven going, the doctors did not believe Samuel would live past birth. But God had a different plan. He lived past birth, spent six months in the hospital, and now lives as a thriving, happy teenager.

My husband and I are extra diligent to keep him healthy due to his small lung size, tracheostomy, and susceptibility to colds and flu. When I read about the outbreak reaching Washington state, I pondered if the virus would travel here. I did not have to wonder long.

Weeks before our local "safer at home" ordinance came into effect, we canceled Samuel's teacher, and his physical and speech therapists. Thankfully, we were able to implement e-learning via Zoom. This left only our nurses coming into our home. I wrestled with the dilemma of allowing anyone in our home; however, the nurses caring for our little guy are a necessity.

My mind went into "what if" mode. What if Samuel's nurses were exposed when they were not at work? How were they handling grocery shopping, meeting with friends, or eating out? What if they unknowingly brought the virus to work? Then I realized I was trying to control my environment and visitors coming into the house. If I could micromanage everyone, then I'd be able to keep Samuel safe. Or so I thought.

The solution to this dilemma? Pray and trust God. This required me to reign in my need to control and, instead, trust God to keep Samuel protected. If I started to worry, I had to remind myself to lean on God and know that He hears the heartfelt call of my momma-heart to protect my special-needs son.

As my county lifted the "safer at home" restrictions and restaurants, retail, and local services opened up, I caught myself thinking about the "what ifs" again. This was exacerbated by my daily viewing of coronavirus news stories. When these weeds of worry cropped up, I applied what I've learned these past few months: Pray, trust God, repeat.

Trusting God requires that I give Him what is most precious to me: my son. Much like falling backward into His arms, I need to trust that He will catch me. When I give up control to God, then He gets the glory by answering my anguished prayers for my miracle boy.

Do not be anxious about anything, but in everything by prayer and supplication with thanksgiving let your request be made known to God (Philippians 4:6 ESV).

21

No Easter Without Christmas

Diana Leagh Matthews

I love Christmas.

At Christmas we celebrate the birth of Jesus and enjoy time with family. However, as I tell my residents at the skilled nursing home where I work, we can't have Easter without Christmas. Before Jesus could become the sacrificial Lamb, He had to be born as a babe in a manger.

Yet, Easter has always held a special place in my heart. It's a reminder of the precious gift Jesus provided for all mankind. The gift of salvation and eternal life.

Working as Activities Director, one of my challenges is to come up with out-of-the-box activities for my residents. The goal is to make events special for them, and Easter played on my mind for months this year. How could I make Easter special and go the extra mile to share Christ's love?

Each year, we enjoy both a secular celebration, with the Easter bunny and an Easter egg hunt, and a sacred remembrance.

In the past, I've sung an Easter cantata Daddy and I put together and performed before his death. Every few years, I dust it off and perform for my residents.

In 2019, we held a Seder meal. Of the two dozen residents present, only one had ever attended a Seder meal before. They all enjoyed it and had new insight into the Last Supper.

After months of mulling over ideas for 2020 and praying about it, I stumbled across the fourteen stations of the cross and the fourteen stations of the resurrection. These were new to me, a Protestant, and I mulled over how to bring them to life for my residents. We were still amid the exhausting Christmas celebrations, as I began planning Easter. For months I worked on the presentations, a little here and there, wondering if it would be finished in time.

With great excitement and anticipation, I looked forward to the Easter celebrations and creating extra memories for my senior adults.

Then COVID-19 threw a wrench into life as we knew it. A month before Easter, our facility became one of many across the country to shut down. No families could visit, and no group activities were taking place. Residents had to remain six feet apart in the halls or outside; many chose to remain in their rooms. The one thing many residents asked for were their daily devotions, which we happily provided for them, thankful for a way to continue to nourish their souls. While we are not a Christian-based organization, I am thankful many of my residents have a hungering for the gospel and a sharing of God's word and His love with them.

How could I take the Easter story and, in five days, simplify it while keeping it manageable (both in time and financially), yet memorable? All my plans for Easter were now up in smoke, but there had to be some way to make it special. Back to the drawing board, and Pinterest, to search for ideas. Pleasantly, I found some wonderfully creative ways to incorporate the message of Easter.

While we had some fun activities, such as decorating hats and creating billboard messages as a treat for their families, the primary focus centered on the heart of the season.

For Crucifixion Week, better known as Holy Week, my team made palm tree bookmarks for Monday, and a chocolate cross for Tuesday. On Wednesday, we gave out a hand with the nail wound and a cross with all the reasons Jesus died for us, both printed and laminated.

Then we provided room-to-room communion on Maundy Thursday and on Good Friday recounted the story of Jesus' last week, using the resurrection eggs. When we finished on Friday, we left a small rock with the reminder that Jesus had been placed in the tomb.

Later in the day, one of our staff dressed as the Easter bunny and visited our residents, putting the biggest smiles on their faces. The smiles were the best payment and we loved to see moods lifted, considering the fact that their families were unable to visit.

But we couldn't leave Jesus in the tomb. After all, He rose from the grave. Hence the reason we celebrate Easter.

So, the following week we celebrated Resurrection week. For Monday we had a small donut with an Oreo cookie attached to resemble the rolled away stone and a sign above which read "He Is Risen." Tuesday brought resurrection rolls, and on Wednesday we had chocolate eggs wrapped in red and a printout explaining the legend of Mary Magdalene and the red eggs. On Thursday I sang "Lovest Thou Me" to the residents in their rooms as a reminder of Peter's restoration. On Friday, we wrapped up the week with a laminated hand with a hole in it as a reminder to not be a Doubting Thomas, along with a cutout of a dove as a reminder that Jesus sits at the right hand of God the father, and His Holy Spirit is with us.

Along with the daily special treat, which they looked forward to, a short Bible lesson, coloring page and word search page accompanied the treat for greater depth and understanding.

That is one Easter I will never forget. It took some creativity, but we were able to provide deeper insight into the meaning behind Holy Week and Resurrection Week for our residents, while not running ourselves ragged. Instead, it became a slower, more contemplative time of pondering and remembrance for all Jesus did when He went to the cross and arose from the grave. We also noticed these creative pursuits opened the doors for greater communication with residents who wanted to discuss their faith, ask questions about salvation, or desired to go deeper in their knowledge of the Bible.

For years, life has become so hectic during the holidays. This year it was nice to slow down and contemplate the true significance of why we celebrate Easter, along with the sacrifice Jesus made for our lives and the true meaning behind this holiday.

Of course, I'm already considering next year. Maybe I'll provide a firsthand account to Jesus' ministry, crucifixion, and resurrection with a monologue from Mary Magdalene.

No, we did not let COVID-19 stop us from celebrating the birth and resurrection of Jesus.

22

Reaching Out

Cynthia A. Lovely

The pandemic has produced unique challenges and situations. In prayer one morning, one particular situation came to mind. I kept thinking about a former friend and wondered how she was handling life through all the general turmoil. I knew her oldest daughter was pregnant with her first child and due in the midst of the health crisis. My friend was very family-oriented and probably had looked forward to being with her daughter in the hospital, praying in the waiting room, and welcoming the newborn.

The reality of the day did not play out that way. Restrictions prevented any hospital visits and the grandparents had to be quarantined a few weeks before they could see their new grandchild.

Even though we had not kept in touch, I felt the burden of her anxiety and worries and continued to pray for her. The still small voice urged me to write her a card of encouragement. "But God," my inner voice queried, "our relationship is strained and we parted on so many misunderstandings. How can I possibly minister to her?"

No thundering voice replied. Just a soft whisper, "Write."

I wrestled with this for a few days and finally sat down with pen and paper. The words flowed. God's anointing kicked in as I reminded my friend of God's faithfulness to her from her earliest years of serving Him. I knew God had worked many miracles in her life and within her family, over and over again. We had been in the same church as teens and had grown up together until life took us on different paths.

I cried over the note, poured my heart into it, sealed it with a prayer and mailed it.

About a week later I received a short thank you card in the mail. Okay, mission accomplished.

Shortly after this, clicking on something online, I found a testimony from my friend that mentioned how much a particular card "from someone unexpected" had ministered to her. It had come at a much-needed time and she felt strongly that it was directly from the Lord to strengthen her and uplift her during the difficult weeks. She read it every day.

I knew it was my card because she actually read part of it online. Again, I cried, thankful my words had touched her heart and boosted her faith. The Lord is so sweet to give me this surprise of positive feedback.

Did it mend our friendship? Probably not. But I didn't expect it to. Yet there was a peace in my heart from obeying the nudge of the Holy Spirit. When God gives us words and direction, our part is to obey, not to question the impact or results. He will accomplish the task.

Especially during this pandemic, I pray we are open to God's calling — in our words and in our deeds. Let us put aside our hurts and grudges and work together to lift up our brothers and sisters in the Lord, and all those around us. We all need encouragement, comfort, strength, and the reminder of God's faithfulness. Break down the walls; be obedient to God's voice.

Do not hesitate to share God's love and promises. Even in something as simple as writing a card.

23
God's Plans vs. COVID-19

Helen L. Hoover

Oh my, how are we going to continue to manage this move? Missouri is going to restrict travel to non-essential next week," I moaned to my husband Larry at the beginning of April 2020.

In the fall of 2019, we had started looking for a place out of town to buy. We believed God was directing this change because we had not expected or wanted to relocate again after our move to Arkansas in 2012. We are in our middle seventies and moving is hard work.

Our family was an hour's drive from us, and the grocery store and other conveniences were only a couple miles from our residence. But we both felt the urge to move.

Small acreage with trees, one-story house, large workshop for Larry, a room for my sewing, paved road to the home, garden space, covered deck, alternate wood heat and an on-site water supply were our requirements. We didn't have a clue where to look, but Larry and I started searching the online realtor sites. When we found something in our price range, we did a drive-by search. If the property looked promising from our drive-by we called a realtor. If not, we continued looking.

We tried not to let frustration overtake us. "God, this seems to be taking a long time to find the right property, but we do want to buy the place you have for us." After five months of looking in three states, driving by about forty homes, and two almost-buys, we found "it."

The place fulfilled our requirements and we both had peace about the property. We began the procedure for buying the property and boxed up everything in our house that we weren't using. The closing for the property was March 6, 2020. By this time we had begun to hear about the COVID-19 Virus, but we didn't think it would come to Arkansas and Missouri to interfere with our move.

The new property was only forty-three miles from our Arkansas home, so we thought we could move a lot of our possessions ourselves in our truck and eight-foot trailer. We would get help from friends and relatives for the bigger furniture.

Instructions for social distancing and wearing masks had been given, but that wasn't a problem for us. We loaded and unloaded the trailer, then stayed in the truck while making the one-day trips twice a week. To avoid any possibility of virus exposure for everone, we didn't encourage anyone to help with the moving.

By the first of April we had enough furniture and food at the Missouri residence to live there, so when the shelter-in-place order came from the governor, we shifted our sleeping and cooking from Arkansas to Missouri.

"God, we ask for Your strength and endurance to continue this move," we prayed. We had some big and heavy pieces of furniture and shop equipment left to move. We wondered if we could do it ourselves, but we shouldn't have wondered since God was directing our move. He took care of our energy levels and wisdom for moving the articles. Furniture sliders, a two-wheel furniture dolly, and a small garden trailer were our helpers.

Exhaustion took over many evenings, but rest brought restored energy and strength to move another load a couple of days later. The end of May found us finished with the moving and ready to list our Arkansas property with a realtor.

We are delighted with our Missouri property. We enjoy listening to the bird songs and watching the butterflies flutter across the lawn. The peace and quiet of this location is relaxing. Daffodils, Iris, Creeping

Phlox, Wild Roses and Redbud Trees have thrilled us with their beautiful blooms.

As we look back on the past three months we wonder, "How did we do it?"

Actually, we know, we didn't do it. God did. We are so thankful for His help, wisdom, guidance and strength.

The COVID-19 scare did not deter God from the plans He had for us.

24

Five Minutes

Patricia Butler

At a picnic table in Shepherd's Park,
we set out our newly minted meal
on weather-beaten planks and sit.

Crackers for communion, wine in tiny jars,
a prayer — at noon, we will observe
five minutes of silence for the poor.

The world isn't listening. Atop the
scaffolding, a construction worker drops
his bucket. A car alarm trips — twice.

Children on a distant boat chatter
like drunk jays in the jasmine. A plane
banks left, then another, and again.

The wind fidgets — blows the crackers
from the table, ruffles the feathers
of the fishing heron.

A husband and wife greet us, entering
the halls of our silence unaware,
picnic sacks in hand.

The wind doesn't stop. A ladder topples.
The traffic hums past a bicycle cycling
past a motorboat passing on the creek.

We can't tell where the wind will gust.
It swallows the jogger's footfalls,
sneaker-quiet in constant motion,

another kind of noise competing with
the wind, toppling buckets, ladders,
communion crackers. Where, Wind,

will you blow next? The Wind's relentless
though the world's not listening. It knows
where it comes from and where it's going.

There is no corner of this city the world
doesn't clog or the wind neglect.
We hear it rattle, disrupt, separate,

hear its deep-down silence, silencing
commotion. We're the startled poor,
on wood planks sitting under pines and oaks,

listening for the Voice
always speaking — stop — the timer dings —
five minutes of silence.

25

More Than a Scrapbook

Marilyn Nutter

When in my first year of college, due to being less active than when in high school, I gained 15 pounds. So did many others, creating what became known as "The Freshman Fifteen." At that time, desserts and snacks were my downfall.

Fast forward fifty years and social media added a new term, "Quarantine Fifteen," as a side effect of the COVID-19 pandemic. Posts from friends lamented too much time at home, snacks within easy reach, and stress eating that added ounces each day and pounds each week.

I was determined not to renew my membership with a different chapter of weight gain.

For me, living alone presented the challenge of social isolation and the temptation to eat. Social distancing meant no visits with friends in a high-risk category, so I had to keep busy. Projects I had put off for another day "when I had time," needed my attention.

I now had time.

I dusted off boxes of photos and slides and sorted memorabilia from envelopes. For days, I reviewed people and events from years past. As one who has chronicled family vacations for the past ten years in commercial books by uploading photos, prints from the past presented an opportunity for scrapbooks.

I devoted one scrapbook to tea. Years ago, I was not the only woman in a large church looking for connections. In response, the women's ministry team offered to organize tea groups where eight women could gather once a month in each other's homes for tea parties. I was assigned a group of strangers who, during the next seven years, became close friends. But there's more. As a writer, I saw biblical parallels to tea and published a book of devotions.

Once I placed the tea photos, party invitations, and information about my devotional book onto the scrapbook pages, I wrote a narrative describing my journey from loneliness to friendship and publication.

I kept my weight down during the pandemic, cleared boxes of photos and memorabilia, and used time to remember and chronicle God's work during a specific time in my life. Scripture reminds us *not to hide these truths from our children; we will tell the next generation about the glorious deeds of the L*ORD*, about his power and his mighty wonders* (Psalm 78:4 NLT).

One day, when my grands sort through my possessions and turn the pages in my tea scrapbook, I want them to know tea was more than a beverage and parties, but a women's ministry idea that bore fruit. God wove friendship in the lives of eight strangers, and my decision to attend removed my loneliness and made a difference in writing devotions to encourage others.

Maybe someday when my grands are struggling, they will remember their grandmother's experience and know God is always at work in our lives in unusual ways.

26

A Birthday to Remember

Diana C. Derringer

*Grandchildren are the crowning glory to the aged;
parents are the pride of their children.*
Proverbs 17:6 NLT

Mom turned ninety years old on April 12, 2020. In February my sister, brother, and I began planning for this special event.

Typically, we don't pay much attention to birthdays in our family. We send cards and occasionally give a gift, but usually nothing more than a special meal. Cake is optional. However, we wanted to make Mom's ninetieth a birthday to remember. So we planned, prepared, publicized, and put Mom on notice. A surprise never entered our minds. That would have been almost impossible to pull off on our sharp-as-a-tack matriarch. Plus, she would have wanted to look her best on such a momentous occasion with all those guests. Her involvement also guaranteed we would invite everyone she wanted to attend.

Although we did not plan a huge affair — a reception at the church with family and friends — the fellowship hall would have been packed, with people spilling into adjoining classrooms and out on the church lawn. As one of eleven children, Mom had enough nieces and nephews to fill the church several times. We knew many would not make it, but we also knew many would. Confirmations came from several states as well as from numerous in-state family, friends, and church members. Mom alternated between her usual "You shouldn't go to all that trouble," and "That will cost too much," to excitement over everyone coming to share her special day.

A few weeks before the big event, almost everything was in order — contacts made, food ordered, entertainment lined up, photographers in place, supplies purchased or borrowed.

And then . . .

We began to hear rumblings about a vicious virus. At first, we paid little attention. Reports from other countries, followed by a few in the United States, caused no personal concern. We prayed for those affected but expected this bug, like others before it, to eventually dissipate.

A few in-state reports caused us to take greater notice.

Mom was the first to express the reservations we were all beginning to feel. When a nephew close to Mom's age was hospitalized in a neighboring state, from an unknown illness with COVID-19 symptoms, she said she wondered if we should postpone the event. In addition to that nephew, many others who planned to attend fell into the high-risk population for the virus.

At that point most public places, including churches, remained open. Nevertheless, we chose to err on the side of caution. We contacted the pastor and the person who prepared the church bulletins to request they undo announcements made the previous week. We also backtracked our other contacts and resolved to make the best of a bad situation.

We considered a small family gathering with the families of Mom's three children, two grandchildren, and three great-grandchildren. However, we soon abandoned that plan as well. None of us wanted to risk infecting one another, especially Mom, with a life-threatening illness.

When May 12 rolled around, Mom's celebration consisted of cards, calls, social media messages (yes, Mom uses social media), groceries set inside the back porch instead of a feast on a table, other drive-by deliveries, and conversations from the front yard while Mom and our brother, who lives with her, sat on the porch.

Were we disappointed? Yes. Do we regret our decision? Not at all.

Birthdays are simply days on a calendar. We did not get to celebrate in the way we wanted that particular day. However, because we chose to keep everyone safe, we look forward to celebrating many more days with this special lady who happens to be our Mom.

We did achieve one goal: Mom's ninetieth birthday will certainly be one to remember.

27
Finding Joy and Purpose

Rebecca Carpenter

The one who listens to me, who carefully seeks me in everyday things and delays action until my way is apparent, that one will find true happiness.

~ Proverbs 8: 34 (Voice)

Swirling mist blurred reflections on the mirrored lake. Minutes later, little clouds dissipated and an up-side-down forest glowed on the water.

Cypress limbs, heavy with last night's rain, drooped like a weary traveler. Water diamonds gathered on the patio screen and waited to twinkle in the sun.

Only a couple of trees in the forest displayed a brilliant green. Shadows subdued the remainder of the woods.

Despite the somber mood, cheerful birds sang melodious tunes. A spider web glistened between limbs of my oak tree.

Isolation brought both favorable and negative consequences. For months, I stayed home alone. Normal activities stopped. My car rested but biking increased. Walking provided daily exercise.

During the pandemic, my time enjoying nature from my patio increased. A collection of birds, from a tiny hummingbird to majestic eagles, appeared. An abundance of vivid flowers graced my garden. My time with God each morning became richer and increased my faith.

After not accomplishing much for a while, I wrote a to-do list. Gradually, the list grew smaller. Along with cleaning the garage and purging files, I read many books, returned to long forgotten crafts, and called to check on friends and family members. The Internet kept me connected but cards and phone calls also helped relieve loneliness. Leisurely days continued for several weeks.

Then Zoom became part of my life with three Bible studies, a writers' group meeting, a writing critique session, and board meeting. Local charities needed supplies so I ventured out to the store. After weeks of free time, suddenly, I needed a schedule.

Life around the lake changed when the sun rose and light replaced shadows. Likewise, opening up our country took me into a new phase.

Living in isolation restyled my life in both positive and negative ways. Although I missed being with family and friends, I enjoyed a less complicated way of life.

Decisions await. Will I return to an often-hectic schedule or cut back on some activities? Will I continue pursuits I actually enjoy or hang on to some out of misplaced obligation? Will I remove the insignificant to concentrate on the significant?

In seclusion, I realized what was most important. Praying for direction, reading the Bible, enjoying people I treasure, and serving with the love of Jesus give me joy and purpose. God takes it all and weaves something beautiful.

Loving Father, thank you for working in my life and revealing your plan to me. Amen

28

Good Friday, Pandemics, and Great Aunt Jorsey

Martha Hynson

My great Aunt Jorsey lived with us when I was growing up. She liked to sit on the sofa, crocheting and dipping snuff. Sometimes I would plop down beside her and listen as she told stories about the olden days. One of those tales recounted the death of her sister, Cinda.

That sounds like a horrific event to describe to a child, but I found it fascinating. You see, according to Aunt Jorsey, when Cinda took sick and died, there were others in the house who had been stricken with the same illness. Those who were well didn't want the sick folks to know what had happened, so they slipped Cinda's body out of the house through a window.

As a kid, I knew nothing about the Spanish flu pandemic that took Cinda's life. The account seemed other-worldly. A far-fetched fable from long ago and far away. It certainly had nothing to do with the life I knew.

To be honest, I continued to see it that way until recent days.

Lately, I've been thinking about it a lot. I wish I knew more details, but no one who was actually there is still alive for me to question. Although the rest of the family survived the flu, everyone in that generation eventually succumbed to one thing or another. Even Aunt Jorsey, who lived into her nineties, ultimately left this earth.

Death is the global health crisis from which no one escapes. We are all infected. We know that, of course, but it's stressful to think about.

So, we distract ourselves in all sorts of ways, attempting to slip that reality quietly out the window. But then something like coronavirus comes along, the world grows dark with death, and we are forced to stay put and think about it.

In a way, it seems appropriate that the observance of Good Friday should occur during this time, when life as we know it has come to a halt. On a much greater scale, that's what happened on the day Christ was crucified. The sun ceased to shine and, in darkness, mankind was forced to be still and contemplate death.

And so it happens, that on Good Friday, 2020, I was doing just that. As I reflected on Jesus and Cinda and COVID-19, I realized that when Aunt Jorsey told the story of Cinda's death, I knew I could believe her, even though it sounded far-fetched, because the one who told me was actually there when it happened.

It occurs to me that I believe the account of Jesus' death and resurrection for the exact same reason. It's the most incredible story ever told, yet I believe the events truly happened because the One who experienced it is the same one who speaks to my heart.

I've been wondering what Cinda's family thought about — in the days and years following her death — when they saw the window her body had passed through. I hope they didn't look *at* it, but rather *through* it. I hope they felt the Holy Spirit speak to them of life in a blade of grass and sunlight dancing through trees.

If a person had never seen those things and someone described them, would that person believe? Is it harder to trust that a tiny seed, buried in the dirt, can grow into a beautiful flower than to trust that the One who created seeds and flowers can lay down his life and pick it up again?

I hope Cinda's family knew that it was only her body they carried out that day. I hope the experience was a picture to them of another window, one that Cinda — as a follower of Christ — simply slipped through to begin her true and eternal life.

29
Adventures at the Doorstep of a Pandemic

Heather Roberts

"Run, run, Grace, get back in the van before they see you! Did you get our homemade hearts on their window? They're going to be so surprised!"

"Yep, Mom. I got them all taped on. Drive, hurry, hurry before they come out the front door!"

As the mother of four — ranging in age from six to fifteen years old — and a pediatric occupational therapist, crafting comes naturally to me. We created stain glass window hearts with tissue paper, clear sticky plastic and construction paper. We spent three hours delivering them in the rain, sun, and wind, with laughter and joy at the thought of the smile on our targets' faces. Giggling uncontrollably makes it hard to stick tape onto our treasures and get them up without being seen.

Reaching someone without touching them, that's a trick. Because I was determined to find the magic formula, and never a person who idled well, my family's adventure began. We made it our personal mission to show people that they were missed, loved, and vital to us, through our deliveries.

Health always starts in the heart. Discouragement, fear, loneliness, and neglect are a greater threat to our wellbeing than a virus and the effects can be life long. COVID-19 attempted to instill fear, create loneliness, and isolate people. We decimated the virus's plans with constant scheming and special deliveries of hope and love.

Our adventure became to find ways to combat this threat of heart sickness with encouragement, love, connection, and joy in the face of a pandemic.

Our speedy deliveries also included colored scripture cards with beautiful artwork. Creations of flowers, made with everything from paper plates to paint and markers, showed up on doorsteps. Smiley faces and little notes were also a favorite delivery of ours. I found gratitude journals to mail to all the women in my immediate family. One friend loved peeps, so we loaded their porch with that sugar-pumped sweet.

Every day I called my mother and father and sent them emails of funny quarantine memes and pictures of the grandkids.

I sent emails to check on my co-workers in the school system, tasked with creating great remote learning and therapy. I educated four children of my own, while learning eight new on-line platforms, and juggling a schedule of tele-therapy sessions.

Discouragement couldn't be an option for me, my children, or anyone I cared about. A smile, a handwritten note, even a wave on a walk, those are the things that touched my heart. As time wore on, we increased our efforts to touch and encourage others' hearts.

Fueled by the love freely given to me by Christ, I did my best to let it flow from me to others. Sometimes hoarding encouragement and love seemed like the logical thing to do, especially on the days my spirit became weary. Yet, God prevails.

My family and I clung to God to keep us afloat. Every morning we started with a devotion. My teens enjoyed the Bible Project via YouTube and the girls watched Minno, a streaming service. The various prayer groups I belonged to, or led, prayed for repentance to sweep our world, for supernatural health and for the awe of the Lord to increase. I know personally that for me and my family our awe of the Lord did in fact increase, granting us our boarding pass to our marvelous adventure.

30
Parting Our Red-Sea Trials

Alice Klies

Could COVID-19 be our Red-Sea trial?

Did you know that "Fear not – do not be afraid" is referred to one-hundred-seven times in the Old Testament and forty-two times in the New Testament? Fear is a common condition for many of us, and it seems to be a priority with God. *Do not be terrified. The Lord your God who goes before you, He will fight for you* (Deuteronomy 31:8).

Because worry, to me, seems as inherent as breathing, I struggle during this Pandemic. I struggle with my own faith and trust, especially since my dearest friend recently had brain surgery for Metastatic Melanoma.

My heart twirled in anguish because her husband couldn't be with her during any of the procedure due to the COVID-19 shutdown. I hurt inside for my friend, who couldn't feel the touch of her husband's gentle fingers stroking her sweet face or holding her close to his chest to reassure her.

I called daily to check on her condition and was always greeted with her husband's soft, tender voice telling me, "She is doing well. I'm fine, and yes, I'm eating In-and-Out burgers every day."

So, here's the deal. My dear friend and her husband breathed through God's promises and never complained. I knelt in awe of their courage while I felt my own distrust and doubt, then shame.

I think I would be screaming to God to part this Red Sea. Right now.

After I've taken a long look at myself, I've asked forgiveness for not trusting that all of this is in His hands and I need to open my Bible and put my trust where it's supposed to be.

A month passed, and the amazing gifts coming out of this Red-Sea trial boggled my mind. Relationships strengthened within my friend's family. Her own anxiety issues had almost ceased because, after all, this is the worst possible thing she never expected. Why worry about the small things? All who know my friend are seeing the miracle God has produced in her outlook on life. Oh, how our Lord devises ways of turning difficulties into deliverances and problems into praise!

For myself? Well, I'm looking at many things differently. I've cut my blond hair short and am letting my natural silver emerge. I'm seventy-six years old and I'm right where God wants me to be so why am I trying so hard to look younger? I haven't yet quit wearing makeup, because that's a little scary to me when I look in a mirror.

I'm grateful to have spent more time at home as meetings and church have been canceled because of COVID-19. My husband may not agree. But he seems to enjoy playing cards or games with me on a daily basis. I've learned how to use Zoom meetings. I joined a group of ladies and helped make 2,020 hospital gowns for our local hospital.

Yes, I'm all about committing my Red-Sea trials and situations to Him, in prayer, trusting Him, and watching Him work wonders. I'm trying to look at this difficult season as an occasion to reflect on the sufficiency of divine grace, and glorify.

When the Hebrew nation stood fearfully facing what appeared impossible, our God parted that Red Sea so they could walk through on dry land to safety.

He can do the same for us, in our Red-Sea trials.

31
You'll Never Know How Much It Means

Jamin Christian Baldwin

We should please others. If we do what helps them,
We will build them up in the Lord.

~ Paul (Romans 15:2 NLT)

I had managed to keep in touch with Miss Mike, as our former neighbor is affectionately known by my family, on a weekly basis after she moved to a different town, and even during the long illness of Ray, her husband. But, after her surgery and change in facilities, several weeks passed before I was able to get in touch with her care provider who gave me her new contact information.

Despite the fact that I was rushing about, running errands and marking things off my weighty to-do list, I decided to give her a call.

The relief I felt at hearing her familiar voice on the other end of the line evaporated as she conveyed her loneliness at the lack of human contact.

The declaration, NO VISITORS ALLOWED, had prohibited Miss Mike from seeing her husband at the VA hospital during the last few months of his life. Denied even the ability to go to his funeral, she was left with a hollow feeling.

Between losing her husband of sixty plus years and the complications with her surgery landing her in the nursing home, she found her days filled with silence. Her one pleasure was what would happen just beyond that solitary window pane.

As our conversation continued, I experienced a mixture of awe and sadness as she told me of the lengths her children were going to, just to see her face:

> At any minute the phone would ring. That was her one connection to the outside world, her thread of hope that tied her to the ones she loved.
>
> Like sunlight surging into her room, she watched the faces of two of her beloved children pop up in the window, looking into her room. Her daughter waved excitedly, pressing her cellphone to her ear.
>
> Her son placed his hand on the glass pane, as if to reach out and touch her. Miss Mike stretched her hand toward the glass. Though their hands did not meet, their hearts did.
>
> Seconds later, her phone rang. Not a sad little drone, but a merry jingle, singing out, breaking the silence.
>
> With a smile, she answered the call.
>
> "Hello." Her children chorused into the receiver. The blessed sound banished the feeling of abandonment and sadness, for a moment. She smiled and returned their wave, as they began their daily visit by phone and on the opposite side of a windowpane.
>
> With all the restrictions being placed on them due to the rapid spread of the sickness, this was as close as her children were able to get to her. They were separated by brick and mortar and glass, but nothing could stop love.

"You'll never know how much it means to me that you called," she told me as our conversation wound to a close.

With the COVID-19 outbreak shutting down the world, I had been guilty of focusing on myself and my own needs. It's easy to forget there are other people adversely affected by this pandemic. Needs are more than a shortage of a few cleaning products, more than the inconvenience of wearing a mask, more than the drudgery of cancelled parties and trips to the movies. I would never have dreamt a few short minutes out of my busy day could mean so much to someone. as it had to Miss Mike.

I realized "you'll never know" what it means for you to call someone to ask if they have everything they need. "You'll never know" what it means that you called just to talk — for them to hear someone's voice break the silence.

Hearing her words replay in my mind, I determined to turn the guilt into productivity. Taking a piece of paper, I made a list of all those who might have been overlooked during this pandemic and determined to make contact with them.

We are to think of others, and help them in their affliction. Perhaps those afflictions aren't simply physically based. Let us broaden the definition in our hearts to encompass those who are lonely — those who are forgotten.

As a wise woman called Miss Mike once told me, "You'll never know how much it means."

32

About That List

Cathy D. Dudley

If I write them down on paper, life's loose ends become more orderly. I'm a seventy-year-old wife, mother, and grammy. For as long as I can remember, I've been making elaborate and colorful lists to help me and my family stay organized: A red heart by an item means top priority; a yellow star is less important but still needs to be done today; something underlined in blue can wait until tomorrow. How else could I remember my appointments and accomplish my many activities? Maybe you can relate.

I often described our young family as a three-ring circus. Although Amy, Sara, and Matthew were born within thirty-seven months, they rarely did the same thing at the same time. My husband and I were co-ringmasters, introducing our dynamic children to the world and keeping the show running smoothly. Yes, we were always busy . . . and yes, there were always simultaneous performances. Our daily to-do list might include anything from happy 4-H horse grooming, enforced piano practice, lively ball games, to a quiet trip to the library, in addition to three completely different sets of homework. It was a hectic, often chaotic time. But the common denominator was always love.

Scripture counsels us to *teach children how they should live, and they will remember it all their life* (Proverbs 22:6 GNB).

These are a few ways to work God-moments into our child's routine:
1. Model praying at meals, and take turns leading the prayer.
2. In dinnertime conversation, talk about how you've seen

God at work in the world. Examples might be a new flower blooming or someone helping another.
3. When you're playing games, include ideas found in Christian activity books.
4. Alternate reading favorite bedtime stories and Bible stories.
5. After a nighttime prayer, turn out the lights and sing "Jesus Loves Me" or "Angels Watching Over Me."

The items on my daily list have changed over the years. Now in retirement, I fill my days with volunteering and other leisure activities. A typical list could involve purchasing construction paper and glitter to teach an art class, biking on my favorite country road, meeting Mother for Bible study followed by putting just one more piece in her jigsaw puzzle, hiking with my husband, working on my newest book, or cutting out puppets for Children's Chapel. It's strange, but I still feel like there's never enough time in the day.

Recently it seems everyone's personal list has become shorter. One by one meetings and fun activities have been crossed off. These cancellations are an attempt to limit the spread of a dangerous coronavirus. People are getting sick. I agree social distancing is a good thing, but more and more my spirits are sinking as less connection is becoming the new normal. I'm not only missing whatever thing was cancelled but also the relationships that are such an enjoyable part of any activity. To be honest, I'm mad at this COVID-19 and resent its power to have such a huge impact on our health and lives.

But I had a beautiful epiphany. The coronavirus has no power over God! It can't cancel our meeting with God, our connection with God, our relationship with God. That's right. COVID-19 can have absolutely no effect on my being with God. God is all-powerful and can't be crossed off a list. As a matter of fact, there's no need to even put morning devotions, Bible reading, and praying throughout the day on a to-do list. Activities with God come about as naturally as holding your child's hand when crossing the street. No scheduling required.

So, although our cancelled activities do have worth and merit, it may be that what is *not* on a list is of highest value. And this is God! The Bible assures us *God is our shelter and strength, always ready to help in times of trouble* (Psalm 46:1 GNB). Yes, our almighty God is available 24/7 and will see us through this coronavirus thing.

Let's be sure our children and grandchildren know about our powerful God who can be trusted to take care of us all the days of our lives. *"I will proclaim your greatness, my God and King; I will thank you forever and ever. . . . What you have done will be praised from one generation to the next; they will proclaim your mighty acts"* (Psalm 145:1, 4 GNB).

Thanks be to God!

33
Duty and Faith

Odell Sauls

Amid the current crisis, I continued my nursing responsibilities.

I'm a Veteran's Administration home health nurse
and must see patients in their homes.
I don't feel afraid as I enter a veteran's home.

What changed in my profession
probably should have been implemented long ago.
I now wear a facemask and don gloves
before entering a patient's home.

I pray every morning before starting my visits.
This gives me extra protection, the kind one cannot see.

Because of my faith, I don't feel fearful.
I'm able to perform my nursing duties
and can empathize with the patients.

God's hands are on me
and I take that strength with me wherever I go.
To serve is a privilege I don't take lightly.

34

7 A.M. with My Dog Freya in the Time of COVID

Laura Sweeney

It's 7 A.M. and Freya Monster, my mini doxie, is throwing a tantrum because she wants to know why she can't have another Oinkie and she wants to know why we aren't on our morning walk yet.

Freya Monster senses something's different. These mornings I don't go to Pilates or to the gym and when we go to campus it is empty, evacuated. Not that I mind the break, or the chalk drawings scrawled on the sides of buildings, like "We Pray 4 U COVID19."

And the blossoming trees, lemon and lilac and lavender, or white as the egrets I spy near the edge of Campus Lake, remind me that life goes on.

But every building is locked, interrupting our routine. Freya usually takes the lead as I follow her through the student center or the music building or Old Baptist Foundation, where I'll sit for a moment and pray. She'll trot up to a door and I will check whether or not we can go in. But these days the answer is always nope.

Since the Great Lockdown, our routine has changed. Instead of me getting up and fetching my bourbon pecan coffee at the bakery, I get up and fix decaf, and steel-cut oats.

Instead of going to the Co-Op for lunch, I prepare a skillet black bean mix, toss in Uncle Ben's Whole Grain Medley, pico de gallo, tuna, or sometimes a thin slice of the last meatloaf I grabbed before the country shifted into shelter-in-place.

Freya sensed something was different when, after two years living in this rented house the fridge — which has been mostly empty — now is stocked to overflowing. The week before the lockdown, she and I went to Rural King, CVS, and Walgreens, me grabbing rolls of paper towels and bottles of hydrogen peroxide that I stacked by the fridge. Freya watched as I unpacked almonds, pineapple juice, tomato sauce, and Parmesan cheese. As the stash spread to include Triscuits, Wheat Thins and Ocean Spray on top of the fridge, extras of her dog food and Greenies and bags of bones on the other side of the fridge, she knew something was up.

Freya knows something is up when I can't sleep nights, the knots wrenching in my stomach from worry about how I will make ends meet after I graduate with nowhere to go. For three years I've been in an MFA coma, limiting distractions, like the news. But now from 3-7 P.M. daily I feel like my civic duty is to tune in to the latest COVID-19 developments, though I try to limit my viewing while I focus on my thesis. And Freya knows something is up as she clings to my shoulder while I Zoom-meet my students. She knows it's her job to support me through these changes, though she's bored, too, that we have nowhere to go.

She misses our shopping trips — especially to TJMaxx. She loved riding around in her tote in the cart while I searched for a dress to wear for my defense or graduation party (though our gala was canceled due to the pandemic). But she likes Walgreens' drive thru. She has always liked drive-thrus, whether she eats the treat the clerks give her or not. She knows she has the cuteness factor . . . like the other day when, as the pharm tech passed my groceries through the drawer, the masked pharmacist peered over the pharm tech's shoulder to catch a glimpse of Freya in my Camry's rear window.

Instacart is different. When someone delivers my groceries, I leave them outside on my front porch for hours before I bring them into the house. Freya watches as, one by one, I wipe each package of yogurt and applesauce and seltzer water and beef jerky with soap and water.

I have to be careful how much jerky I feed her; it upsets her tummy. And maybe I am too lenient about her Oinkies. But she is cooped up too, tolerating my mood fluctuating day by day.

Easter Sunday, when I used my oven for the second time in the two years we have lived here, Freya knew something is different. I made a pineapple upside down cake after finally getting two cartons of eggs at Walgreens along with oil and yellow cake mix. I had already stashed the pineapple though it was pineapple chunks, not rings. Freya watched eagerly as I prepared the mixture. Then she licked the bowl for the forty minutes the cake baked in the oven, until her collar was soaked in batter.

Yes, Freya knows something is different. Like when we go to the soccer fields, or I stare too long at the yellow caution tape wrapped around the playground, or the social distancing signs cautioning how to stand six feet apart — the length of a long yoga mat or a bicycle. Or when we walk to the tennis courts to look for tennis balls and everything is chain locked.

Still, she gives me that nudge each morning to get up and start our day. No, we are not out and about, Freya and Laura, the coolest chicks in Carbondale. We are hunkered down at home.

And we need our morning walk more than ever.

35
Pandemic

Carolyn Fisher

Pandemic has many meanings.
With each one there comes some fear.
It's the "not knowing what will happen"
To things, and people we hold dear.
It's an epidemic, something that reaches far,
Not only to our families, our friends and country
It's a culmination of things bizarre.
No one seems sure where it started,
Or even where it began.
They prefer playing the blame game.
Was it a country, or an ordinary man?
Lives have been lost. The count is out of sight.
We need a vaccine to get through this,
and they all would rather fight.
It's an illness, a disease; it needs to go away.
We want things like they used to be
So, our kids can go out to play.
Baby killing is not part of God's Plan.
Nor are all the broken homes
where seldom there is a man.
Children need mommies and daddies too.
Fight for your families, so they stick like glue.
Instead we're seeing earthquakes, floods,
Pestilence upon us that we can't comprehend.
Jesus said He's coming soon; this could be near the end.
There's a message in all this, and we need to lend an ear.
It's time for us to get on our knees and pray.
God has spoken, and He has made it very clear.

36

God Thirsts

Bob Blundell

Amid the unprecedented suffering that has ravaged our country with the COVID-19 pandemic, I find myself seeking, with an almost manic hunger, any tiny glimmer of light in the news to give me balance. I shouldn't need moral reinforcement, as I am a Christian and I rejoice and welcome the return of our Savior. But I am also a flawed human being, and like many others I pray this terrible disease will soon pass, and life will return to some semblance of normalcy.

I recently discovered an article in a nationally known publication that offered numerous ways to cope with the social distancing and fear that we are all struggling to deal with. Some of the recommendations included watching award-winning movies or reading the books you've never had time to get to. There were hobbies suggested such as scrapbooking, crocheting, and origami (I had to look that one up). Of course, exercising was on the list and one could relax in a bubble bath with a nice glass of wine. There was even a suggestion to look at photos of puppies (hmm?).

While many of these activities certainly have some appeal, there were some fundamental elements the writer overlooked.

There were no suggestions for us, as a society, to drop to our knees and ask God for direction through this quagmire of pain and suffering. I didn't see a recommendation to thank God for the many blessings we have received, or a call for us to perform corporal acts of mercy for those less fortunate than we are. The most important item conspicuously missing from this list was a single word: Prayer.

I respect others' rights to not believe, but if there's a light at the end of the tunnel for us, it will come through a recommitment to the One who gave us life. In recent years we have taken steps to exclude God from our lives. We have kicked Him out of our schools and sporting events. Church attendance has declined by seventy percent over the last fifty years. Pornography and adultery are all alive, well, and flourishing here in the United States.

Our core values have "evolved." What is accepted now may have shocked previous generations. We have normalized deviation via our tolerance or apathy to a point where few can remember what normal looks like.

I wonder what God must think as He looks down upon His people. Do tears form in His warm expressive eyes as He sadly watches our actions and sees our thoughts? Perhaps.

But I believe Jesus stated His desires very clearly as He spent His last moments on the cross. His simple words conveyed a powerful message when He said, *"I thirst."* Our Savior wasn't speaking in the literal sense. He wanted us to know He thirsts for us, for our love.

That's a humbling concept. After all, we are all so flawed and He is so perfect. But He wants us to thrive and succeed, as spoken in Jeremiah 29:11: *"I know the plans I have for you," declares the Lord. Plans to prosper you and not to harm you, plans to give you hope. . . ."*

I believe even as God gave us free will to make our own choices, He may be saddened to see us step further and further from the ways He taught us long ago. If there was ever a message of infinite love and forgiveness to give us hope, it was told in Luke's gospel in the story of the Prodigal Son. In this parable, the father rejoiced when his wayward son returned to him, despite having committed grievous sins and rejecting him.

We have become modern-day prodigal sons and daughters through our actions, beliefs, and our tolerances, often seeking fulfillment through means other than Him. But God is waiting for us to return.

God the Father thirsts for us now. He loves us completely and waits for us with open arms.

I wonder what the world will look like when we emerge from this health crisis. Will we quickly seek normality as defined by what we've known, done, and thought in recent years? Or will we use this time and these events to turn back to Him. To observe and practice what He told us was the most important concept in life.

You shall love the Lord, your God, with all your heart and all your soul (Matthew 22:36).

I pray we use these times of fear and suffering as an opportunity to reexamine our thoughts, our actions, and our values, and to recommit to the One who created us. We might all take that first step by kneeling and offering Him a prayer of thanks.

37

We Got Married

Alexis Conrad

We got married.

Nick and I married after COVID-19 descended upon my community.

We got married without my best friends standing next to me, or his groomsmen beside him.

We got married without most of our extended family present to celebrate with us.

We got married despite not having a salon open to get my nails done. I didn't get my eyebrows fixed, or have a professional hair and makeup stylist.

We got married without a band or DJ, fancy dinner or incredible venue decked out to a T.

Instead, our family surrounded us for a peaceful, wonderful day. We had time to laugh, relax, and enjoy each other. My sister flawlessly applied makeup to my face and attached artificial nails to my fingers. She decorated the ceremony site with simple, yet romantic items.

My sister-in-law brought candles and my grandmother-in-law arranged flowers just the way I wanted them, without stress or pressure.

My children stood with us. Dad, dressed in his suit, lovingly walked me down a garden path as a makeshift aisle while my soon-be-husband fumbled with music from his phone. All I could do was smile.

I shared this special moment with my best girl, my daughter. Nick drove the half-mile to my parents' house, giving my daughter and me a few tender moments to walk home through the woods together from the garden ceremony site, hand in hand in our long-flowing pearl-colored dresses. Neighbors said they contemplated whether fairies were emerging from the woods. Pure and magical — and one of the most special moments of our lives — like something from which fairy tales are made.

Mom decorated her beautiful front porch with lights and glittering gold accents, and we shared pizza and cake while social distancing.

We spent our time enjoying the day. Things didn't have to be perfect . . . but somehow, they were. We had the most perfect and dreamlike day without all the trimmings we had thought we needed for a wedding.

Turns out, we don't need those things for a wedding to be meaningful, beautiful, and romantic. Our love made this day perfect. And we danced the night away.

Our wedding day was perfect because we said our vows to each other while standing in front of the garden cross and before God.

I wouldn't have changed a single thing.

38
Glorifying God in a Global Pandemic

Becca Wierwille

When the country shut down in March 2020 due to COVID-19, so many of my plans for the spring crumbled before my eyes.

I'd been preparing fun end-of-year activities for my kindergarten class, but now we were navigating murky waters of learning online. I'd finally signed with a literary agent, but now I was worried about the state of the publishing industry as it transitioned along with the rest of us.

My husband Seth and I had hoped to start house hunting, but now realtors weren't allowed to show houses. While we didn't see any effects of the virus in our immediate circles, our challenge was to discover our "new normal."

Every peek at social media sent shivers down my spine. I turned to Seth, my calmer counterpart, asking him again and again, "What now?"

Of course, Seth didn't have any more answers than I did.

Spending quarantine in our small apartment was rather unappealing. We decided to stay with my parents for a bit to enjoy the open spaces of their farm while everything else was shut down. The problem was, at the farm, it was easy for me to put the virus out of my mind entirely. I stopped listening to the news, stopped reading articles about the virus, and stopped thinking about all the suffering.

While that may have made my life easier, my avoidance of reality was probably a little unhealthy. My life had changed, but everyone's life had changed in one way or another.

Some were like me, adjusting to a new normal of working at home and wearing masks to go to the grocery store. Others were using quarantine as a chance to rest and practice self-care after years of rush and hurry. Some were trying to balance parenthood with teaching, while their children resisted the idea of the home as a classroom. Others were sick or knew people who were sick. Some were stuck at home alone, completely isolated, starving for interaction and yet knowing they must stay inside for at least a few weeks longer. Others were out of work and struggling to put food on the table. Some were watching their businesses slowly ebb away. Others weren't sure how they would make it out of the pandemic at all.

My perspective was limited. There is always more going on than what hits closest to home.

While I didn't want to be selfish and stuck on my own relatively small issues, I still felt removed from those who were far more affected by the virus and state closures.

Then one Sunday a few weeks in, during an online worship service, the pastor preached on Psalm 67. In this big-picture passage, the writer focuses on all nations and all peoples praising God.

I wanted this psalm to be my prayer, too. I didn't want to be so focused on myself that I missed the big picture: that God's glory would be known in all the earth.

Even in the midst of a global pandemic, God is with us. God is sovereign and mighty and He has the power to end the most contagious virus with a single word. And so, in whatever happens, our biggest concern shouldn't be what we want most. Our biggest concern should be God's glory.

At the end of the sermon on Psalm 67, the pastor asked, "How can we pray for God to be glorified in all that is going on?"

We want to pray big, bold prayers. We want to pray for miracles, because we serve a miraculous God. And yet, even as we pray our biggest and boldest prayers, let's never forget to pray most of all for God to be glorified. Because in the end, He is all that matters. He is the one who has conquered the grave. He is the overcomer.

I bookmarked Psalm 67 in my NIV Bible, and I've been praying it almost every morning since: *May God be gracious to us and bless us and make his face shine on us–so that your ways may be known on earth, your salvation among all nations* (vv. 1-2).

> God's grace is in every day. He still gives us so much more than we deserve, even when life is hard. I want His goodness to be known by everyone, because He is what we truly need in this broken world.

May the peoples praise you, God; may all the peoples praise you. May the nations be glad and sing for joy, for you rule the peoples with equity and guide the nations of the earth (vv. 3-4).

> God is with us, and He guides us. Even if He doesn't answer our prayers the way we expect or hope, we can be glad and sing for joy, just to know His presence.

May the peoples praise you, God; may all the peoples praise you. The land yields its harvest; God, our God, blesses us. May God bless us still, so that all the ends of the earth will fear him (vv. 5-7).

> God blesses us, but we need to open our eyes to see His blessings because they often are not blessings by the way the world defines them. Whatever happens next in this global pandemic, may God be glorified, so that all the people of the earth will come to know and love Him.

And after life returns to normal, as our masks are removed and our homes are again opened to our neighbors, may we never forget how God was, and is our shelter, our savior, our healer, and our protector — no matter the earthly outcome.

39
All Shall Be Well

Jeri McBryde

I realize there is a lot in this nightmare world of the coronavirus that I cannot control. One thing I can do is quit watching the news where I am being told non-stop that older people with chronic medical conditions should stay at home. That they are at higher risk of contracting COVID-19 and a higher risk of not surviving.

I hit all the buttons: age seventy-three, compromised immune system, heart problems, cancer, etc.

My family has put me in lockdown. For once I look forward to doctor visits just to get out of the house. Sitting in the backyard among the birdfeeders, soaking up the sun, and listening to the wind chimes blowing in the breeze has become a delightful part of my day. I have learned the names, the songs, and habits of the colorful cardinals, finches, mockingbirds, hummingbirds, woodpeckers, Carolina chickadees, and blue jays that join me.

I call my friends. Often, I am the only voice they hear for days. We are all lonely, in our seventies, eighties, and nineties. We miss our Senior Water Aerobics class and Taco Fridays. We compare our aches, pains, and our fears. Each of us has lost someone to this pandemic or know someone who has tested positive. We pray that God will comfort us.

Amazon has become my new best friend. Shopping online is a new adventure.

I have a new hobby: I count toilet paper rolls and cleaning supplies. Keeping my freezer full and my cupboard stocked with canned goods is a top priority. I'm getting so good at it my son and daughter know where to come when they run out. We meet at the end of the driveway, masks on and six feet apart.

I am getting old — as the news continues to remind me — and at high risk for severe symptoms including death. I de-clutter a little bit each day. While cleaning out a closet, I came across boxes of letters and files containing genealogy research my father started twenty years ago. After he died, I put it aside.

When my cousin called to check on me, I told him of my find and we began reminiscing about our childhoods. He mentioned I was now the oldest living member of our family. When I am gone, our history will be forgotten.

Today with the computer, information is more accessible. I have decided to continue the genealogical journey for my granddaughter and future generations. I am no longer lonely. I am surrounded by pictures of my ancestors, reading the stories they shared so long ago. My days are now full.

God is in control and all shall be well.

Jeremiah 29:11 assures us, *"I know the plans I have for you,"* declares the LORD, *"plans to prosper you and not to harm you, plans to give you hope and a future."*

40

The Field

Mindy Gallagher

Winter brought brisk adventures as my childhood friends and I filled the field with snowmobile paths. In the spring it was a place to run wildly around, spinning, dancing, laughing, falling. And by mid-summer its tall grasses hid me from the rest of the world, providing a private sanctuary where I could be alone with my thoughts.

So much more than just a few acres of grass, the field held my secrets, my passions, my pubescent tortured soul. Here I discovered I could be my true self, entirely free. It was *my* field.

In 1972 my life as a fourteen-year-old girl was a continuous rollercoaster ride that swept from one dramatic event to the next, ad infinitum. The small town in which I lived had next to nothing to offer in terms of entertainment. No bowling alley. No movie theatre. Not even a McDonald's. Summers seemed especially interminable.

At this time, I was madly in love with Joey Moretti, whose big Italian family resided about three miles from my house. Despite the sweltering June heat, Joey rode his bike up every day to hang out with my friends and me. Our favorite meeting spot was a small, non-working dairy farm about half a mile down the road from my neighborhood.

When I was a child this farm had been a place full of adventure for me. There had been kittens to name, cows to help herd in from the pasture every day at three o'clock, and calves from whose backs we were thrown more than once. But by 1972, all that remained was the farmhouse, and across the street from it, the field.

It was in this field that we roamed, smoking cigarettes, telling stories, exploring new paths —being youths. Joey and I cultivated our deep love for one another as we walked hand in hand through the tall reeds and grasses.

Junior High in the 70s consisted of seventh and eighth grade; high school started in ninth. In the fall of 1972, I became a freshman in high school and Joey, being a year younger than me, remained at the junior high. Though we tried to make our relationship work "long distance," it proved to be too challenging for our young hearts. By mid-fall we broke up, and I was devastated.

I took to the field for solace, and it did not disappoint.

Joey was my first real boyfriend, but not the last person I brought to the field. Through the years I would introduce every new interest to this serene, comforting place tucked away from the rest of the world. I felt that to understand me, one must understand this field and the meaning it held for me. It had become my personal oasis. Among its charms was a large, gently sloping hill on the north side, punctuated by a sprawling oak tree that leant shade and support on hot afternoons. Oh, the hours I spent alone under that tree, writing poetry and songs, pouring my adolescent heart out on paper!

Fast forward several years to when college was behind me and I was starting down a career path. With every trip home to see my parents I still made sure to visit that field. It somehow grounded me. Walking through it, or along Jasper Street (which separated it from the farmer's property), instantly stirred passions tamped down by what was now life's rigid schedule. I was once again a young girl, full of dreams and creativity. I breathed in the earthy scent of dead and living foliage mingled together, filling my nostrils with an indescribable lushness.

Here was peace.

The first time I came back after the bulldozers started demolishing my sanctuary, I was heartbroken. Homes were going up, new roads were being forged, and my oak tree was gone.

There were new green street signs with names like Benjamin Drive and Whitney Street leading to unfamiliar neighborhoods with seedling trees and freshly sodded lawns. Jasper Street was the only piece in the landscape that held to its original form. I imagine that by now it, too, has been repaved, refined, and perhaps widened. I don't know. I've not wanted to go back and check. I prefer to hold the field in my mind's eye just as it was. Pure, vast, unwavering in its allegiance to me, allowing my unfettered, imperfect self to exist among its small hills and valleys without judgment.

Recently, I found myself a bit shaken when on a Sunday morning I learned that four members of my band and two singers would be unable to participate in worship due to a possible COVID-19 diagnosis. For me as the worship leader, it was already challenging to work with the echoey sound in the gym where we'd moved to allow for social distancing. Suddenly, the reality of the day and age in which we're living struck me, and I felt helpless and out of control. The already mounting discouragement continued to grow as I realized I would be leading worship from my keyboard with only a drummer and one other singer as backup that morning.

I got into the shower and lifted my voice to God. As I did, I felt my attitude changing. From deep inside me words of peace sprang up. Hope began to replace despair. In that moment this truth became clear: God never changes. Hebrews 13:8 tells us *Jesus Christ is the same yesterday and today and forever.* The same God who gave me strength to lead worship back in our sanctuary with a full band is still on the throne. Surrounded by all my equipment and the myriad of musicians I hadn't fully recognized how much I needed Him — and how much He is actually in control.

I've come to realize something about my field as well. Indeed, it was a place I could run to for acceptance and peace, but it was not sustainable. It changed. The truth is, for a period of time God gave me a field, something beautiful and tangible where He could reveal

Himself. It brought me exactly what I needed as a young teen. But as lovely as it was, it couldn't last. And in reality, it wasn't my sustainer anyway. He was. In the middle of the tall grasses when I cried out — it was God who actually met me. The peace I felt? He gave it to me. He knew me then just as He knows me now, just as He has always known me: imperfect and in need of a Savior.

He's ready to lead me through all the uncertainties I face if I will only take His hand.

Today I look back on my life and see many fields. Gifts of time, friendship, beautiful landscapes, creativity. In the midst of each stands a single being: Jesus Christ, my hope and peace forevermore.

The grass withers and the flowers fall,
but the word of our God endures forever.
Isaiah 40:8 NIV

41

Give Me Liberty, or Give Me... COVID?

Jenny L. Cote

Like a tyrant sweeping across the globe, COVID appears to have taken control of everything and everyone. We all have numerous stories of what the virus has taken from us. For some, it has taken lives. For others, it has taken livelihoods. But for all, it has taken liberty.

I'm a children's historical fiction author and have labored for over a dozen years researching the American Revolution. I'm passionate about instilling a love for America's founding history into young people. I have the American flag painted on my toenails year-round, for crying out loud!

My favorite day of the year is Independence Day, and I bleed red, white and blue. So in today's divided climate where our history is being maligned, torn down and left untaught, I feel the call to tell America's true story for the next generation. I zealously seek to inspire kids to fall in love with America and that "precious jewel of liberty" as Patrick Henry called it. As The Voice of the Revolution, Mr. Henry rallied a nation to independence with seven little words, "Give me liberty, or give me death!" But as the tyrannical virus closed in on America during March 2020, my voice would soon whimper, "Give me liberty, or give me COVID?"

I had made great plans to launch my new book, *The Declaration, the Sword, and the Spy* in April 2020, replete with interviews, book signings, visits to schools and homeschool groups, and appearances at historical sites. But instead of being in person at Lexington and Concord where the first shots of the American Revolution were fired, COVID forced me to zoom virtually into history with the rest of the world. I was crushed to see my plans evaporate in a matter of weeks. Like King George III bullying the colonies, so the invisible little COVID beast seemed to call all the shots, or so it would have you believe. And it was only getting started.

For over twenty years my family has been blessed to have a home at beautiful Lake Burton in the North Georgia Mountains. This is a place of weekend retreats and solace, of summertime fun and refreshment. And of course, the best day of the year is July 4th when docks are festooned with enormous American flags and red, white and blue bunting. Each year I dress up as Lady Liberty to go view the fireworks out on the lake, giving my best *Titanic* pose on the front of the boat and holding my lighted torch high as we glide past honking boats and smiling patriots. But COVID had other plans for Lady Liberty this year.

When the lockdown came, my husband and I decided to essentially relocate to the lake house full time. If we were stuck at home, why not be stuck where we could get outside and go for a boat ride, take a hike in the mountains and socially distance on the dock? We ran back into Atlanta once a week for groceries and mail, so we wouldn't bring potential exposure to the locals in Rabun County. We took every precaution to avoid COVID at the lake . . . but it came to us, nonetheless.

In mid-June, we had a friend up to the lake house for one night. She was due to have surgery so she came for a last bit of summer fun before going under the knife. When she went in for her pre-op visit, they routinely tested her for COVID. She was positive but asymptomatic. That soon changed for her — and for me.

I was on an exciting conference call about new plans to make my first novel into an animated feature film when I started feeling warm. Within an hour after hanging up, I had a 100.4 degree fever and felt like I had been hit by a truck. I've never had body aches like that! I climbed into bed, and my husband donned his mask and tried to keep his distance as he sanitized the house. We decided to head back to Atlanta the next day to quarantine and be near medical attention should I need it. I ordered an at-home COVID test kit that arrived the next day, and within forty-eight hours I was confirmed as positive. The tyrant had me by the throat.

My fever and body aches only lasted forty-eight hours and then suddenly vanished. I had no symptoms for the following two days, which lulled me into a false sense of security. *Well, that wasn't so bad!* I thought to myself. But, COVID is a really weird virus. I liken it to a ball in a pinball machine that goes in every direction with no rhyme or reason. New symptoms arrived — malaise, metallic taste, and difficulty drawing a deep breath . . . but no real cough to speak of. All I wanted to do was sleep, so I took my zinc and Vitamins C and D, drank OJ, and stayed in bed. Thankfully, after two weeks the symptoms lessened.

As July 4th approached, I was feeling better but still not up to par and was unwillingly to be around family until I tested negative. While they all traveled to Lake Burton for BBQ and fireworks, I sat at home pouting. Lady Liberty's crown was knocked off and COVID sat there in my quiet den, smugly mocking me: *I took your book launch, your health, and your favorite day of the year! I've taken away your family, your readers, and your opportunities. And I've taken away your precious jewel of liberty. I'm wearing your crown now!*

Not so fast, tyrant.

I suddenly heard loud noises and stepped outside to walk up my darkened driveway. To my surprise and delight, I was encompassed in a symphony of liberty! A cascading waterfall of red, white, and blue fireworks drifted down from a neighbor who ignored the rules and took liberties to celebrate America. Others soon joined in, letting their fireworks explode in every direction. The pent-up frustrations with restrictions from the previous months seemed to burst in defiance overhead.

I stood alone in my cul de sac and wept tears of joy to realize I was not alone at all on the 4th of July. My fellow Americans enveloped me in the sights and sounds of liberty, and filled me with such joy. I stood there thanking God for this gift, and for those who refused to allow anything to keep them from liberty.

Smiling, I went to sit on my screened porch, lit candles and listened to the distant fireworks that continued for hours. God then spoke to my heart. *No tyrant can take away the liberty I give. Nothing is allowed to touch you unless it first comes through Me. You are my child, so trust what I allow for your highest good, and My greatest glory. The Enemy seeks to destroy anything to do with truth, freedom and liberty, but I alone wear the crown of sovereignty. This tyrant's attempts to take these things from you will be turned for good in ways you cannot yet imagine, but will see in the days to come.*

Nothing is allowed to touch you unless it first comes through Me.

I was suddenly reminded of something I read by F. B. Meyer. He explained that at night shepherds of old would gather their sheep within a high-walled area and sleep at the gate. If a wolf wanted to get to the sheep, it first had to go through the shepherd. And the shepherd had his rod ready to beat the terrorizing beast away. Jesus called Himself the Good Shepherd. Nothing can touch you that He hasn't first allowed to pass by Him, including even loss. Only He knows the full picture of all that is transpiring in every single life, and will use all things for our highest good and His greatest glory.

As Jesus began His ministry, He visited His hometown synagogue of Nazareth where He read from the scroll of Isaiah: *"He has sent Me to heal the brokenhearted, to proclaim liberty to the captives. . . ."* (Luke 4:18).

Whatever COVID the tyrant has taken from you, Jesus longs to restore in abundance to you in unexpected ways if you will trust Him. He will heal your broken heart. He will proclaim liberty over your captive life, and set you free. You may not be able to envision it now, but give it time. Every tyrant, including COVID, must fall to the King of Kings.

I'm happy to report that God didn't need my help to launch my new book. *Because* of COVID, my online book sales are soaring. *Because* of COVID, my animated movie dreams are unfolding faster than I could have imagined or planned. *Because* of COVID, I have been able to share the gospel with unbelievers who are gasping for hope and the true liberty of salvation in ways I couldn't before the lockdown.

Whose crown has been toppled now, you smug little invisible tyrant?

Lady Liberty will don her green foam crown next year for July 4th. Meanwhile, she'll allow the King of Kings to wear the real crown and topple her tyrants any day of the year.

* * *

John 14:1 NLT
"Don't let your hearts be troubled. Trust in God, and trust also in me." ~Jesus

John 14:27 NLT
"I am leaving you with a gift - peace of mind and heart. And the peace I give is a gift the world cannot give. So don't be troubled or afraid." ~Jesus

Hebrews 4:16 NIV
Let us then approach God's throne of grace with confidence, so that we may receive mercy and find grace to help us in our time of need.

Psalm 46:1 NIV
God is our refuge and strength, always ready to help in times of trouble.

About the Authors

Jamin Christian Baldwin is an award-winning devotion writer from Southeastern Ohio. Her devotions have been featured on christiandevotions.us, as well as many blogs, as a guest author. She is an active member of the ACFW-Ohio chapter. She enjoys mixing photography and poetry, which she shares on Instagram: instagram.com/jaminchristianbaldwin. Her personal devotions can be found on her Facebook author page: facebook.com/jaminchristianbaldwin.

Bob Blundell has published in magazines including *The Bible Advocate*, *Liguorian*, *The Living Pulpit*, and *The Compass*. His work also appears in *Remembering Christmas Moments*. Bob and his wife, Dee, live in Friendswood, Texas.

Patricia Butler is a poet, writer, and pioneer in missional arts, cultivating a global network of artists through mentoring, writing, and teaching. She has lived in New England, France, Italy, and Atlanta, and is now based in South Florida, where she enjoys boatyards, the arts, and walking with cranes. Pat has three chapbooks. New projects include three manuscripts and blogging at www.mythicmonastry.org.

Rebecca Carpenter enjoys writing at her lakeside retreat near Orlando. After she retired as an elementary teacher, she and her husband traveled to all seven continents. Some journeys were mission trips and others were for pleasure. Experiences with her granddaughters, traveling, and nature inspire her writings which have appeared in Focus on the Family's *Clubhouse* and *Clubhouse Jr.* magazines, *Christmas Moments, Cool-inary Moments,* as well as other publications. After her husband, and both parents passed away within a year, her writing focus changed. Writing about grief and God's presence filled page after page. Friends encouraged her to write a book to help others. Forty devotionals are included in her book *Ambushed by Glory in My Grief.* Visit her at http://rebeccacarpenter.blogspot.com.

Alexis Conrad graduated from college with a BA degree in psychology and uses this practical knowledge to assist her as a wife, mother, and real estate agent. Additionally, she assists her mom with Shine Camp — a summer camp designed to empower teen girls to live by biblical principles. Alexis is passionate about her family, photography, the beach, and lazily resting in a hammock.

Karen Cook renewed her love of writing this year with the encouragement of her husband and two high school daughters. She is grateful for her Word Weavers group cheering her on!

Jenny L. Cote, award-winning author and speaker, developed an early passion for God, history, and young people. She beautifully blends these three passions in her fantasy fiction series, *The Amazing Tales of Max* and *Liz*® and *Epic Order of the Seven*®. Likened to C. S. Lewis by readers and book reviewers, she speaks on creative writing at schools, universities and conferences around the world. Jenny has a passion for making history fun for kids of all ages, instilling in them a desire to discover *their* part in HIStory. Her love for research has taken her to most Revolutionary sites in the U.S., to London (with unprecedented access to Handel House Museum to write in Handel's composing room), Oxford (to stay in The Kilns, the home of C. S. Lewis, and interview Lewis' secretary, Walter Hooper at The Eagle and Child, the famed pub where the Inklings met), Paris, Normandy, Rome, Israel, and Egypt. She partnered with the National Park Service to produce Epic Patriot Camp, a summer writing camp at Revolutionary parks, to excite kids about history, research and writing. Jenny's books are available online and in stores around the world, as well as in multiple e-book formats. Jenny has been featured by Fox News on *Fox & Friends* and local Fox Affiliates, as well as numerous Op-Ed pieces on FoxNews.com. She has been interviewed by nationally syndicated radio and print media, as well as international publications. Jenny holds two marketing degrees from the University of Georgia and Georgia State University. A Virginia native, Jenny now lives with her family in Roswell, Georgia.

Laura Craft loved writing everything from adventure tales to humorous stories about animals as a child. As an adult, our loving Father surprised Lauren with chances to use her favorite pastime every day. To her joy, Lauren has been published in more than a dozen Christian book compilations and has held a journalism post for the past thirteen years. As simply a messenger of good news, Lauren finds joy in sharing about the abundant life Jesus promises His followers

(John 10:10), filled with eternal hope, unconditional love, rest for the soul, and lasting purpose. She lives in Virginia. You can connect with her at laurenchristianauthor@gmail.com.

Diana Derringer is an award-winning writer and author of *Beyond Bethlehem* and *Calvary: 12 Dramas for Christmas, Easter, and More!* Hundreds of her articles, devotions, dramas, planning guides, Bible studies, and poems have appeared in more than 40 publications, including several anthologies. In addition, Diana writes radio drama for Christ to the World Ministries. Her adventures as a social worker, adjunct professor, youth Sunday school teacher, and friendship family for international university students supply a constant flow of writing ideas. For a free copy of Diana's "Words of Hope for Days That Hurt" and her weekly *Words, Wit, and Wisdom: Life Lessons from English Expressions*, join her mailing list at dianaderringer.com.

Cathy D. Dudley is an author of Christian books for children and their families. She has written *Toddler Theology ~ Childlike Faith for Everyone* and *Faith, Family, & Fun ~ Monthly Lessons to Color and Connect with God's Love*. Cathy lives in the Blue Ridge Mountains of Virginia and is a member of Roanoke Valley Christian Writers. She thanks God for giving her the words to write and invites you to visit cathyddudley.com.

Loretta Eidson loves writing romantic suspense. She's won contests and has been a finalist and a semi-finalist in many others. Loretta is agented by Tamela Hancock Murray of the Steve Laube Agency. She is a team member with the Suspense Squad, and a member of ACFW, RWA, FH&L, SinC, and HACWN. Loretta also serves on the executive and general board of the Mid-South Christian Writers Conference. Loretta lives in North Mississippi with her husband Kenneth, a retired Police Captain. When she's not writing, she enjoys reading, cooking, and spending time with her family. She loves chocolate, caramel. chai tea and coffee. Connect with her at lorettaeidson.com, facebook.com/loretta.eidson.7, twitter.com/lorettajeidson, instagram.com/lorettaeidson/, and suspensesquad.com.

Carolyn Fisher is a widow after 54 years with the love of her life. She resides in Independent Living and is active in her church and residential community. She has published two books, *If You Can't, God*

Can, and *The Tea Set.* She also enjoys painting and writing requested poems for special friends and occasions.

Mindy Gallagher works part time as a church worship leader/music director, and part time at being retired. She is pursuing all of her life-long passions including painting, sewing, reading and writing. She and her husband moved from the frozen fields of Minnesota to the golden beauty of South Carolina in 2018 and are enjoying a whole new adventure.

L. C. Helms is a licensed mental health counselor in private practice in Central Florida. She is also a writer and blogger and has previously published poetry and non-fiction articles under the pen name Carol Lorin. She enjoys writing devotionals, women's fiction, short stories, blogging, and walking alongside others. She is currently editing her novel. You can connect with L.C. on her Facebook author page, @LC Helms Author, Twitter @LChelmsauthor, Pinterest @LCHelmsauthor, and on her counseling website Lorihelmscounseling.com. Her author site is at LCHelms.com.

Melissa Henderson, an award-winning author, writes inspirational messages in articles, devotions and stories. Her first book for children, *Licky the Lizard,* was released in 2018. She is a contributor to the compilations *Heaven Sightings, Remembering Christmas* and *Divine Interventions: Heartwarming Stories of Answered Prayers.* Her passions are helping in community and church. Melissa is an Elder, Deacon and Stephen Minister. The family motto is "It's Always a Story with the Hendersons." Follow Melissa on Facebook, Twitter, Pinterest and at melissaghenderson.com.

Gwen Hinkle is a writer and blogger. Gwen and her family, enjoy living out in the country on a small hobby farm in Oregon. The joys in her life are family and friends and she stays busy working as a home health nurse. But, most of all, she loves to laugh and have fun! Visit Gwen at GwenHinkle.com.

Helen L. Hoover and her husband are retired and live in southern Missouri. Sewing, reading and knitting are her favorite pastimes. However, pulling weeds from the flower and vegetable gardens and helping her husband with home repair receive priority on her time. Visits with their children, grandchildren and great-grandchildren are treasured. Her devotions and personal articles have been published in *Word Aflame Publishing*, *The Secret Place*, *Word Action Publication*, *The Quiet Hour*, *The Lutheran Digest*, *Light and Life Communications*, *Chicken Soup for the Soul*, and *Victory in Grace*.

Penny L. Hunt, award winning author, speaker and blogger, enjoys writing for both children and adults. Her writing has appeared in *Chicken Soup for the Soul*, *Guideposts*, *The Upper Room*, almost every edition of the *Short and Sweet* series, and online in *Just Eighteen Summers*. Her most recent book, *Bounce! Don't Break . . .* helps others bounce back quicker from setbacks. *Little White Squirrel's Secret-A Special Place to Practice*, is an Amazon.com bestseller children's book dedicated to her severely autistic granddaughter. Living in the rural peach growing region of South Carolina with her husband Bill, a retired career naval officer and attaché, and their two dogs, Penny enjoys gardening and gourmet cooking. Her greatest passion is to lead others to a personal and intimate relationship with Christ. Visit her at PennyLHunt.com.

Martha Hynson has loved books for as long as she can remember and is eternally grateful for a mother who read to her. Her greatest joys include reading to her own children and grandchildren, as well as kindergarten and first grade students, and seeing the lightbulb come on as children unlock the reading code. Martha's words have appeared in numerous magazines and publications, including *ParentLife* and *Chicken Soup for the Soul*. She is thankful for her husband, Paul, who would rather watch football or go hunting than curl up with a good book, but manages to listen, and appear interested, as she talks about what she is reading or writing.

Lily Jenkins is an Assistant District Attorney for the State of North Carolina. Her job supports her writing habit. She enjoys writing legal suspense fiction about a smart and sassy female lawyer taking on a powerful syndicate in her small, supposedly sleepy mountain town. She's the newly married wife of Jamie, a super smart cyber-security whiz. Lily and Jamie enjoy swing dancing, enjoying the outdoors, and playing video games.

Sherry Diane Kitts, originally from southwest Virginia near the Blue Ridge Mountains, has lived in central Florida for the past 22 years. She and her husband enjoy their tropical lifestyle and living between Florida's East and West Coast beaches. Sherry began writing short stories and devotions after her retirement, and has been published in several anthologies. She belongs to Word Weavers International and received a Loyd A. Boldman award at the Florida Christian Writers Conference. Sherry creates colorful stories from her life experiences and weaves in biblical truths to reassure others of God's constant love.

Alice Klies has written since she could hold a pencil. She is president of Northern Arizona Word Weavers, a chapter of an international writers group. Through their encouragement Alice began submitting her work for publication. She has nonfiction and fiction stories published in twenty anthologies. She is an eight-time contributor to *Chicken Soup for the Soul* books and has articles published in *Angels on Earth, AARP* and *Wordsmith Journal* magazine. She has been featured in the *Women of Distinction* magazine. Alice's novel, *Pebbles in My Way,* based on her testimony, was released in 2017. In addition to her involvement in Word Weaver's, she is a deaconess and Stephens Minister in her church. Alice, a retired teacher, resides with her husband and two Golden Retrievers in beautiful Cottonwood, Arizona. She prays her stories cause a reader to smile, laugh, or cry, and most of all turn their eyes to God who loves them.

Yvonne Lehman is founder and former director of the Blue Ridge Mountains Christian Writers Conference for 25 years and Blue Ridge Novel Retreat for 12 years. She is author of 59 novels and is compiler and editor of 16 books in the *Divine Moments* Series. Her latest novels include the *Secrets in Savannah Series* (*The Caretaker's Son, Lessons in Love, Seeking Mr. Perfect*) and *The Gift*. One of her most popular novels is *Hearts that Survive — A Novel of the Titanic*.

Cynthia A. Lovely is a freelance writer from upstate New York and a reporter for the *Good News New York* magazine. She has been published in *Chicken Soup for the Soul* books, in *Catholic Forester, LIVE, Sasee*, and in national magazines, *Tea Time* and *Romantic Homes*. She has completed a women's contemporary novel and is working on a Christmas novella.

She is a member of American Christian Fiction Writers, and a staunch supporter of Blue Ridge Mountains Christian Writers Conference. Cynthia is forever grateful for the God-gift of her husband, along with the gain of a lovely signature. www.cynthialovely.com.

Evelyn Mann is a stay-at-home mom who lives near Tampa, Florida raising her special needs son, AKA the "Miracle Mann." She has published her memoir, *Miracle in My Living Room, The Story of a Little Mann* and a devotional, *Thriving Through Your Trials, Devotions of Miracles, Faith & Prayer*. Receiving inquiries from around the world, Evelyn offers other families hope and encouragement, showing that a negative diagnosis is not beyond God's reach. You can read more stories on Evelyn's blog at www.miraclemann.com/blog.

Diana Leagh Matthews is a vocalist, author, speaker, life coach, amateur historian and genealogist. She has been published in many of the *Divine Moments* books. In her day job, she is an Activities Director. She currently resides in South Carolina. Visit her at www.DianaLeaghMatthews.com and www.alookthrutime.com.

Jeri McBryde loves sharing her life experiences in the *Chicken Soup for the Soul* series with the hope of helping others. Her stories have appeared in nine *Chicken Soup for the Soul* books. She has been published in the *Divine Moments Remembering Christmas*. Her works also appears in three anthologies. Jeri lives in a small southern delta town. Retired, she spends her days reading and working on her dream of publishing a novel. A doting grandmother, her world revolves around faith, family, friends, and chocolate.

Fran Braga Meininger writes personal narrative and the blog, *The Years Beyond Youth*, about a time in a woman's life that can be vibrant, fulfilling and engaging despite, or perhaps because of, what comes with age. Her work has been featured online at *Ladies Pass It On*, *Ruminate Magazine* and as a contributor to KQED Public Radio's program, *Perspectives* and *Sixty and Me*; in print in *Sage Woman* and *Valley of the Moon* magazines, as well as in an anthology the *Finding Light in Unexpected Places*. Fran has lived in Sonoma Valley for 60 years and now makes her home in Glen Ellen.

Andrea Merrell is an associate editor with Christian Devotions Ministries and LPC Books, a division of Iron Stream Media. She is also a professional freelance editor and a finalist for the 2016 Editor of the Year Award at BRMCWC. She teaches workshops at writers' conferences and has been published in numerous anthologies and online venues. Andrea is a graduate of Christian Communicators and winner of the 2017 USA Best Book Awards. She is the author of *Praying for the Prodigal*, and *Marriage: Make It or Break It*. For more information, visit www.AndreaMerrell.com or www.TheWriteEditing.com.

Terri R. Miller is an Alabama girl who loves gardening, cooking and bird watching in her backyard. She lives with her husband of 34 years and their Boston terrier, Gabby. Terri has worked in the technology arena for 23 years, but her real passion is writing about the moments in life that connect us to God and to each other. You can follow her blog by going to Life Is Moments. You can also find Terri on Instagram (terri.r.miller) and Twitter (@TRMiller322).

Marilyn Nutter, of Greer, South Carolina is the author of three devotional books: *Tea Lovers, Dressed Up Moms,* and *Diva Delights Devotions to Go*. She is a contributor to *Feed Your Soul with the Word of God* and *The Power to Make a Difference* Bible studies, and *Moments, Prayer: Approaching the Throne of Grace,* and *Perseverance* compilations. She has written for *Power for Living, Christian Living in the Mature Years, Focus on the Family* and *Hope-Full Living*. A Bible teacher and speaker for women's and grief groups, Marilyn serves on the women's ministry team at her church. A grandmother to eight, she smiles and says her cup runs over when they gather around her table. In her life's seasons, she has met God's faithfulness and clings to Lamentationa 3:22-23. Visit www.marilynnutter.com to find treasures in unexpected places.

Stephanie Pavlantos is passionate about getting people into God's Word. She has taught Bible studies for fifteen years and has spoken at ladies' retreats. She is ordained with Messenger Fellowship in Nashville, Tennessee. Stephanie works for Besorah Institute for Judeo-Christian Studies in the Student Services department as well as teaching online classes. She is published in *Refresh* Bible study magazine, *Charisma* magazine, and CBN.com. She is also a contributor for Faithbeyondfear.com, VineWords.net, and *Feed Your Soul with the Word of God*. You can visit her blog at stephaniepavlantos.com and other social media sites at twitter @DPavlantos and facebook.com/stephaniepavlantos. Her Bible study *Jewels of Hebrews* will be released in December 2020. Married for 27 years, she and Mike have three children, Matthew, Alexandria, and Michael. Stephanie loves animals and has dogs, ducks, goats, and chickens.

Heather Roberts is the mother of four energetic children and the wife of an amazing husband. She loves to craft, read, and write. You can find her on her website HeatherN.Roberts.com**.** There you will find simple devotions birthed from real-life reliance on Jesus, encouragement in your daily walk, and of course laughter. Lots of laughter.

Odell Sauls is an RN who enjoys writing. She is a member of the Tampa branch of Word Weavers International, a Christian writers group. She won first place in the Florida Tapestry Awards of 2019 in the poetry genre. A devotion she has written was published in *Inkspirations Online*. Currently, Odell is finishing her first novel.

Joanne DiRienzo Schloeman enjoys writing about life. "My Pandemic Play" is her first published article. She is grateful to her Lord for the gift of a creative mind. Joanne is a member of Word Weavers International and is currently working on a children's book. Her passion is working with families. She enjoys hiking with her husband, crafting, photography, playing the piano, volunteering in her community, and finds joy in assisting her husband, a pastor, with prep for children's sermons. She and her husband live in Arizona.

Ann Peachman Stewart lives in Ontario, Canada and writes both fiction and non-fiction. Her passion for positive, respectful eldercare is reflected in her weekly blog, found at smallmiracles.online where she supports all who care for elders. She is Mom to three amazing adults and a proud grandma of five granddaughters. She is owned by a dog named Teddy.

Gina Stinson is busy reclaiming every day for God's glory after years of living in fear and defeat. She is a pastor's wife of 27 years and homeschool mom. Between family and ministry, she enjoys dabbling in gardening, crocheting, and playing music on her second-hand baby grand piano. She writes true stories of God's reclaiming power and is a storyteller for those who have overcome their circumstances and embraced God's goodness. Her first collection of storytelling devotions, *Reclaimed, the Stories of Rescued Moments and Days*, is due to release in November, 2020. You can find her at: ginastinson.com, or on facebook at: facebook.com/reclaimingeveryday/.

Laura Sweeney facilitates Writers for Life in central Iowa. She represented the Iowa Arts Council at the First International Teaching Artist's Conference in Oslo, Norway. Her poems and prose appear in fifty plus journals in the U.S., Canada, Britain, and China. Her recent awards include a residency at Sundress Publications Firefly Farms, a scholarship to the Sewanee Writers Conference, and participation in the Kaz Creative Nonfiction Conference. During the pandemic she can be found online participating in a virtual Christian writer's conference.

Carrie Vinnedge believes happiness is an act of kindness in written word and afterwards a lovely walk with God.

Becca Wierwille is a kindergarten teacher and writer living in Pennsylvania with her husband Seth and their dog Georgia. Becca's short stories have been published in numerous magazines and anthologies, including *BALLOONS Lit. Journal*, *Guardian Angel Kids* Online Magazine, *Short Kid Stories*, *Flash Fiction Magazine*, Mount Union's *Calliope* literary magazine, and the *Blessings in Disguise* anthology. She is a member of American Christian Fiction Writers and Word Weavers International. Visit Becca at beccawierwille.com to learn more and to read her inspirational blog.

www.ingramcontent.com/pod-product-compliance
Lightning Source LLC
LaVergne TN
LVHW051501070426
835507LV00022B/2875